THE SWEENEY TODD
Shock'n'Roll Show

by Randall Lewton
and Peter Miller

Evans Plays
London

PRODUCTION NOTES

STYLE

Although the play parodies the Victorian melodramas on which it is based, it is full of anachronisms and contains musical numbers far removed from any Victorian style. Therefore there should be no sign that the cast are anything but serious in their performances. If the actors appear to be sending themselves up, the humour will be much diluted.

STAGING

The Fleet Street scenes need minimal scenery, although a doorway must be suggested - preferably two. If tabs are available these can be used for the Fleet Street scenes, allowing the other sets to be prepared out of sight of the audience, although this is by no means essential. The stage plans for the sets as described in this script are included at the back of the book. There is no reason why an excellent production should not be based on just the few basic essential pieces of furniture required by the script - doorways, TODD's chair, tables and chairs for the Gin Palace, a few blocks to represent cellar walls and the exploding pie machine. If more elaborate facilities are available then there are opportunities to create full sets - particularly useful for the climax of the Gin Palace scene and for the gruesome cellar in which most of Act Two takes place.

EQUIPMENT AND EFFECTS

There are several ways in which TODD's chair can be constructed:

a) A simple solution is to place a chair on castors which can be pulled from behind through a curtained section of 'wall'.

b) A simple revolving panel can be constructed. The chair and a section of 'wall' are attached to a small platform which is spun from the rear.

c) The most effective method is to attach the chair to an L-shaped wooden base which is hinged to the floor of the stage. As the chair is tipped backwards the 'floor' comes up to fill the gap through which the chair has disappeared.

d) The coward's way out is to fade the lights and let the actor exit in the normal way in the darkness. This is the least fun and there will always be someone who can see the supposedly murdered body walking out on his own two legs!

Version (c) is illustrated overleaf.

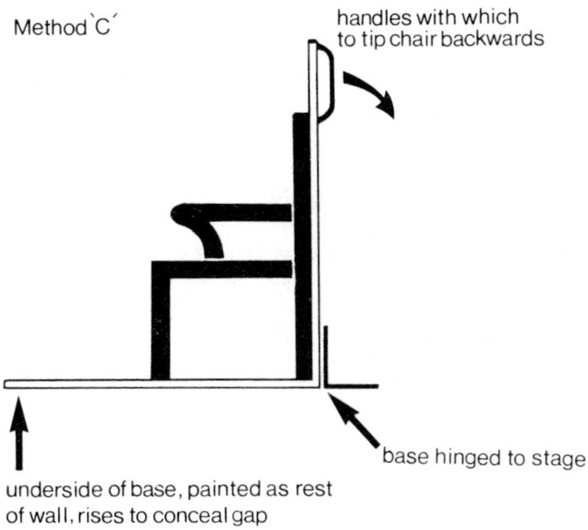

TODD's Chair (c)

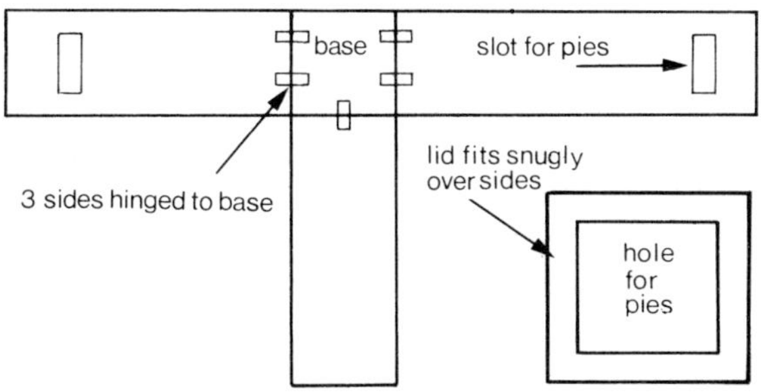

The Exploding Pie Machine (Exploded Plan!)

The first essential is a good loud BANG! Maroons of various sizes are available from theatrical suppliers and are not expensive. Use the biggest one you dare! Properly handled they are harmless!
The machine itself is simply constructed and foolproof in operation. To a base large enough for the OPERATOR to stand on are hinged the front and sides of the machine - it has no back. They are held up and together by a lid which slots over the top of them. It is like a biscuit-tin lid but with a hole in the middle through which the ingredients can be thrown in and the pies thrown out. When the OPERATOR gives the lid a quick hard blow it should fly upwards, allowing the three 'walls' to fall outwards. The sides SL and SR should have holes in them through which the pies can be fired.

The pies themselves can be made from cardboard, plaster of Paris, foam rubber etc. The essential thing to remember is that the ones that are likely to hit anyone should be as light as possible and the ones that are actually going to be eaten should be edible! For the stack of pies (P.54) use foam rubber cut-outs with a string running through the middle, holding them together.

For the 'Thick as Thieves' number a collapsing chair is required. An ordinary wooden chair should be demolished and re-assembled using brown sticky paper. This is just strong enough to hold the chair together as it is lifted but it will tear allowing the chair to fall apart when it is jerked sharply.
This song also requires a knife to stick in the wall. Two knives are needed here. MRS LOVETT pretends to throw the real knife, concealing it as she does so. Seconds later the second 'dummy' knife appears to stick in the wall. It is in fact just a handle and a small section of blade fitted into a piece of the 'wall' to lie flush with it. A wire is attached at the rear and when this is pulled sharply the knife snaps into position. There should also be an appropriate thumping sound. The timing of this effect is vital and it needs to be carefully rehearsed. When it is performed properly the effect is startling!

The ALONZO/FOOZLE hat trick is explained in the text.

LIGHTING

One or two spots are useful if other lighting is limited. For the mad-house song as many disco-style effects as the budget can stand should be used. Rapidly changing coloured filters in the follow-spots as they sweep randomly about are very effective.

CAST

The size of the CHORUS (CITIZENS, NEWSPAPER BOYS, GIN PALACE CUSTOMERS, LUNATICS, POLICEMEN, GHOSTS etc) can vary according to the wishes (and energy) of the producer. We suggest a minimum of six but, generally speaking, the more the merrier. At least two separate groups of chorus singers will be necessary.

The play was originally performed by an all male cast but in this edition it has been adapted for a mixed one. If an all male cast is used to perform the play the following alterations should be made:

a) MRS LOVETT becomes MR LOVETT. This involves only a few small and obvious changes in the dialogue and lyrics.

b) QUEEN VICTORIA becomes a drag role, as in the original production.

c) The following smaller parts can be played equally well by actors or actresses - PICKPOCKET, CITIZENS OF LONDON, GIN PALACE

CUSTOMERS, MADHOUSE INMATES, NEWSPAPER SELLERS, CHILDREN in the Gin Palace, PIE-MACHINE OPERATOR, HECKLER, GHOSTS and ORLANDO.

d) The theatrical tradition whereby the part of TOBIAS is played by a girl can be abandoned and the part played straight. The necessary cuts and alternative lines can be found below:

Page 5

NEWSBOY   Well, I wish you luck, mate.

(NEWSBOY leaves. TOBIAS starts to sob loudly. TODD walks out of his shop and strikes him.)

TODD   Be quiet!. You squealing bundle of rags. (continue with text)

Page 80

TOBIAS   ...... I have no master and no money.

BILLY   I return at once to Kent to marry my sweetheart, Susan. You may come and work on the farm with us. You shall be like a son to me.

TOBIAS   Father! (goes to BILLY)

FOOZLE   Come, Orlando, our master is dead. (continue with text)

PROPS LIST

ACT I

CHARACTER	PROPERTY	SCENE
NEWSBOYS	newspapers	1
	'MEANWHILE' notice	1
PICKPOCKET	2 watches and 2 wallets	1
TOBIAS	bundle on a stick	1
	banknote	1
	bowl of shaving soap and brush	2
TODD	articles of Apprenticeship and pen	1
	razors	2
	piles of clothes BILLY's and ALONZO's	2
	£40 in banknotes	3
	'RESERVED' sign	3
ALONZO	a case marked 'THE AMAZING ALONZO' in it: 2 bowler hats, a jug of 'disgusting, sticky goo', a gold sovereign	1
FOOZLE	a dog collar and lead	1
	half a bacon sandwich	1
	'THE AMAZING ALONZO' case	2
TOMMY	parrot on shoulder	1
BILLY	string of pearls	2
GROVEL	dog bowl, mug of cocoa and tray	3
GILBERT	walking stick	3
CUSTOMERS	glasses, mugs, large jugs labelled 'GIN'	3

ACT II

CHARACTER	PROPERTY	SCENE
NEWSBOY	newspapers	5
TOBIAS	sailor's hat	2
TODD	razor, cord and pistol (not revolver)	5
	ball and chain	5
FOOZLE	'THE AMAZING ALONZO' case with contents	5
PIE MACHINE OPERATOR	pies	2

MRS LOVETT	notice 'NEXT BATCH OF PIES READY IN TEN MINUTES'	1
	pies	1
	bag of flour	2
	'human leg and other items' on a tray	2
	knife	5
ANGELO	pie (hot)	2
	stack of pies	2
	jug of water	2
	silver medal of Saint Peter	5
BILLY	a piece of sacking	2
BEDLAM	a large padlocked box full of gold coins	3
	a large ledger book	3
	a handbell	3
POLICEMEN	guns and handcuffs	5
VICTORIA	a bag full of medals	5

****

STAGE PLAN

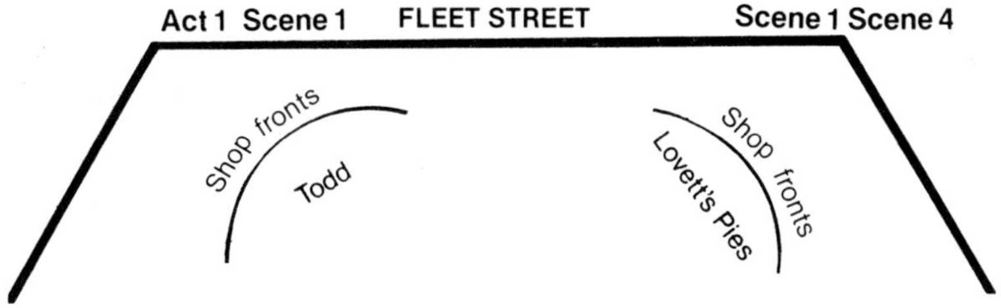

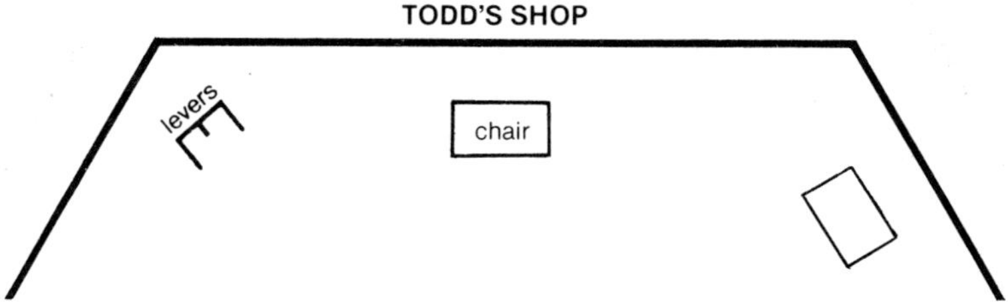

Scene 3 PICKLE'S GIN PALACE

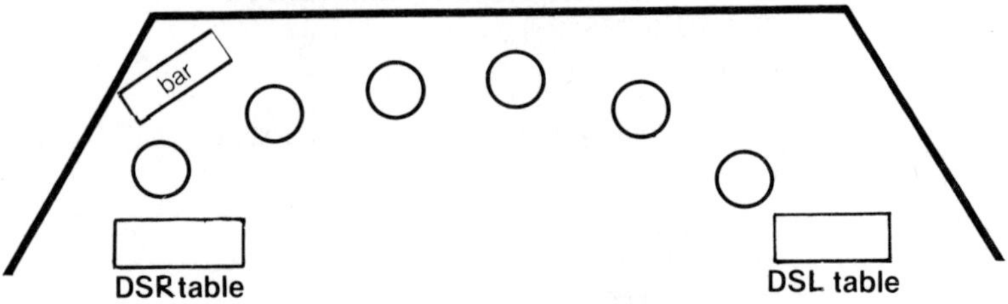

Scene 2 Scene 5 BAKE HOUSE

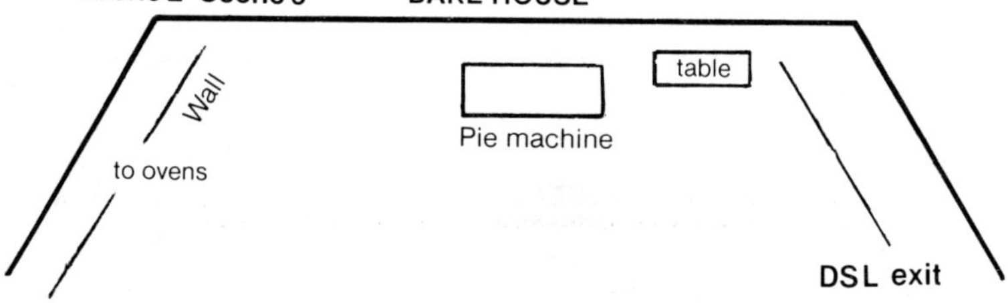

MAD HOUSE AT PECKHAM

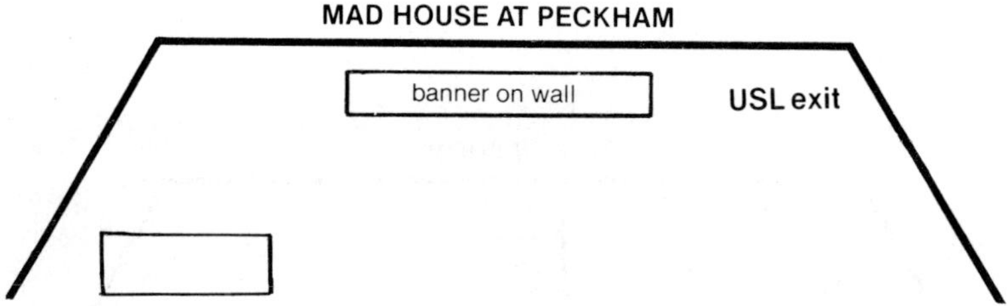

SWEENEY TODD was first presented at Alsop Comprehensive School, Liverpool in January 1979, with the following cast:

Lee Alderdice
Andy Billinge
John Brightley
Noel Briscoe
Christopher Brown
Ian Brown
John Calland
Brian Comyns
Timothy Evans
Martin Finnigan
Ed Franklin
Gary Frew
Derek Hignett
Michael Hill
James Hughes
Phillip Johnson
Colin Jones
Timothy Joslyn
Stephen Lundberg
Keith Mansfield
David Marshall
John McCarthy
Thomas Mitchell
Sean Moore
Alec Mosey
Stephen Nelson
Mark Paterson
Brian Robinson
Graham Smith
Alan Spencer
Peter Swindells
David Wills

and with the help of:

Stephen Barwise
Ian Berry
Paul Bolger
Chris Buckley
Douglas Cashin
Robert Chambers
Ken Cridland
Chris Dawson
David Foden
Stephen Griffiths
Philip Grove
Jeff Hockenhull
Ann Joslyn
Gary King
Vera Lewton
George Lucy
David Mitchell
Alice Pedder
Alan Pevely
Stephen Quinn
Harold Scanlan
Harry Weatherley
Christopher Whittle
Roy Williams

DRAMATIS PERSONAE

SWEENEY TODD, the Demon Barber

TOBIAS STOUTHEART, his Apprentice (who is not all he seems!)

MRS WILHEMINA LOVETT, a Pie-maker

ANGELO, her Italian Assistant

BILLY, a jolly Jack Tar

TOMMY, his Shipmate

THE AMAZING ALONZO, a Sorcerer par excellence

FOOZLE, the Sorcerer's Apprentice

ORLANDO, the Sorcerer's Faithful Hound

POLICE CONSTABLE, a Bobby or Peeler

BEAUJOLAIS PICKLE, brother of Branston, Gin Palace Proprietor

QUEEN VICTORIA, Monarch of the Realm

HRH's ATTENDANT, possibly Gillie Brown of Balmoral

NAPOLEON BEDLAM, Keeper of the Madhouse at Peckham

GROVEL, waiter at the Gin Emporium

GILBERT, an AGA (aged gin addict)

The OPERATOR of the Pastriacci Pie-making Machine Mark III

A HECKLER, who meets with a fitting end

A young and pretty PICKPOCKET

A bored NEWSBOY

and numerous MADHOUSE KEEPERS and INMATES, NEWSBOYS, GHOSTS, CITIZENS of London, short POLICEMEN and two VICTIMS ..... from the audience!

The action takes place in Victorian London

ACT I
Sc.1 Fleet Street
Sc.2 Inside the Barber Shop
Sc.3 PICKLE's Gin Palace

ACT II
Sc.1 Fleet Street
Sc.2 The Bakehouse
Sc.3 The Madhouse at Peckham
Sc.4 Fleet Street
Sc.5 The Bakehouse

*THE SWEENEY TODD SHOCK 'N' ROLL SHOW

ACT I

Scene 1 Fleet Street

MUSIC 1 Sinister music. A single spotlight reveals TODD's shop door USR. A CITIZEN enters DSL crosses the stage. As he passes the shop he rubs his chin as if he is in need of a shave, decides to go in, enters shop. Pause. Suddenly there is a very loud scream. The spot snaps out.

After a short pause bright lights come up to reveal a busy street scene; MRS LOVETT's Pie Shop USL, TODD's Barber Shop USR.

MUSIC 2 If You're of a Nervous Disposition

CITIZENS If you're of a nervous disposition,
If a horror story makes you shriek.
If Crippen, Hyde and Jack the Ripper scare you
Our show tonight will make your knees go weak.

(several NEWSBOYS run on from L and R)

NEWSBOYS Shock! Horror! Hold the front page!
Revelations! Villains low!
Shock! Horror! Public outrage!
A fearful and barbaric show!

CITIZENS We tell a tale of blood and gore and terror
Of a wretch who cared for neither man nor God.
Who kept a grisly, grim and gruesome secret,
A vile, vicious villain - Sweeney Todd!

ALL Shock! Horror! Hold the front page!
Revelations! Villains low!
Shock! Horror! Public outrage!
A fearful and barbaric show!

CITIZENS This Sweeney Todd acquired a taste for murder.
His business grew on theft, deceit and lies,

With his partner working in the neighbouring pie shop,
The customers might eat or fill the pies!

So be prepared for shock and consternation.
If you faint when you see blood you'd better go.
If you've brought your Granny, send her round the alehouse,
Then you'll be welcome to our horror show!

ALL Shock! Horror! Hold the front page!
Revelations! Dealings low!
Shock! Horror! Public outrage!
A fearful and barbaric,
Cheerful, atmospheric,
Tearful and hysteric
Show!

(CITIZENS gradually exit going about their business until only one CITIZEN and a young girl PICKPOCKET are left on stage. The PICKPOCKET looks up and down the street then lets out a blood-curdling yell and falls to the ground. The CITIZEN rushes over to her.)

PICKPOCKET Aaaaaah!

CITIZEN 1 Whatever is the matter? Let me help you. Where is the pain?

PICKPOCKET Oh! oh! Here, ah!

CITIZEN 1 (bending over her) This is terrible! Let me help you up. There's a doctor just along the street.

PICKPOCKET (straightening) No, no. It's all right. The pain's easing now. Just one of my turns. I'm perfectly all right now.

CITIZEN 1 Are you sure?

PICKPOCKET Yes, yes. Thank you kindly, sir.

(The CITIZEN leaves, PICKPOCKET examines the

wallet and watch she has stolen. As another CITIZEN enters she doubles up again. CITIZEN 2 rushes to help.)

(louder than before) Aaaaaaah!

CITIZEN 2 — Heavens preserve us! Allow me, madam. What ails you?

PICKPOCKET — Aaaaaaaaaaaaaaah! (jerks and twitches)

CITIZEN 2 — (kneeling) Courage, madam. Wait here, I will fetch a doctor.

PICKPOCKET — (jumping up) No need, sir. I assure you I am well now.

CITIZEN 2 — The lord be praised. I thought you were done for, my dear lady. A miracle indeed, madam.

(CITIZEN 2 leaves the stage. The PICKPOCKET again examines what she's stolen. SWEENEY TODD enters DSL, PICKPOCKET goes into same routine.)

PICKPOCKET — (louder than ever) Aaaaaaaaaaaaaah!

(She performs a long series of jerks and twitches with accompanying shrieks and groans. TODD stands and watches. Finally the PICKPOCKET lies still, exhausted.)

TODD — Is something wrong?

PICKPOCKET — Oh the pain!

TODD — Oh, I see. A pain. (walks away)

PICKPOCKET — Oh, sir. Help me for the love of God.

TODD — (turning) I do little for the love of God, girl.

PICKPOCKET — If you could just help me to my feet, sir.

TODD — You are a tiresome person. Oh, very well.

(TODD lifts the PICKPOCKET to her feet. She starts to walk away feeling in her pockets for her loot and looks angrily at TODD who is holding up a watch. She walks up to TODD and is about to speak when he silences her with a glare.)

PICKPOCKET (aside) Curses! I know this man. It is Sweeney Todd. I sense that he is a greater villain than I. (exit DSR)

TODD A foolish girl to try and pick the pocket of Sweeney Todd. Yes, I am Sweeney Todd, the finest barber in London town. Here is my establishment. Note the inscription. It is in Latin. I am also a great scholar. Freely translated it reads 'Hair today, gone tomorrow'. My little joke, you know. MY LITTLE JOKE, YOU KNOW! But I have no time to waste talking. It's time that my shop was opened. You will see that my razor is as sharp as my wit!

(He goes into the shop. TOBIAS enters wearily DSR carrying a bundle on a stick and sinks to the ground in front of TODD's shop. A NEWSBOY enters USL, his head buried in a paper. He trips over TOBIAS.)

NEWSBOY You clumsy oaf!

TOBIAS I am sorry. I was so weary that I could not take another step. I have walked for three days to reach London.

NEWSBOY Hardly seems worth it. What did you want to come here for?

TOBIAS It is a long and tedious story.

NEWSBOY Oh well then .....

TOBIAS But if you insist I will tell you the whole tale.

(A violin plays mournfully in the background - sound effects department. The NEWSBOY yawns and leans against convenient wall.)

Until last week I lived a good and happy life in - (local district). Since my father died when I was a baby my mother and I have lived in a simple way. We were poor but we were honest. Alas our honesty did not protect us from our evil landlord. We were thrown out to fend for ourselves in the cold, cruel world. My mother was overcome by the shame of our situation, took ill and last Thursday evening - oh, I weep to think of it - she died in my arms.

NEWSBOY (awaking from doze) Yes, well ... (starts to leave)

TOBIAS Before she died .....

(NEWSBOY leans on wall again.)

..... she gave me this. (produces banknote) It was all she had, and she told me to seek an apprenticeship here in London.

NEWSBOY And I hope you .....

TOBIAS For three days, an orphan, I trudged on weary feet through mud and foul weather until I reached this place. I have had nothing to eat, little to drink and my clothes are rags. I can go no further - and I'm only little.

NEWSBOY You are starving, are you? You have a five pound note there. Buy yourself a dinner with that.

TOBIAS No! This banknote is all I have in the world. I must keep it as long as I can. If I spend this then I am doomed to poverty and starvation.

NEWSBOY I'd keep that money in your pocket if I were you. There are some funny characters about, you know. Well, I wish you luck mate. (makes a quick exit)

TOBIAS (to audience) There is more to my story than I dared to tell a stranger. ('he' removes cap to reveal beautiful long hair) The world is a dangerous place for a young girl, alone, without a friend or protector. This disguise has deceived all those whom I have met on my journey and now I hope it will enable me to find a home and earn a living .... (she replaces the cap tucking in hair) ... although I must confess I am at a loss to know where to begin my search. I am lost and weary and the wind stings through these ragged clothes. I started my journey with strength and a confident heart but now .... now ..... I think constantly of my poor mother and my heart grows heavy.

(She sobs. TODD opens his shop door to see who is making the noise, sees TOBIAS and walks out and hits him.)

TODD — Be quiet! You squealing bundle of rags. Are you trying to drive away all my customers? (aside) I have few enough as it is.

TOBIAS — Forgive me, sir. (looks at the shop) You are a barber, sir?

TODD — <u>A</u> barber? The <u>finest</u> barber in London. In the world

TOBIAS — An honest trade which I would be proud to learn.

TODD — What do you mean, boy?

TOBIAS — If you should need such a thing as an apprentice, sir, I would be a credit to you, sir, I promise you, sir, if you would take me on, sir.

TODD — (aside) He is a weak and miserable specimen. Yet I might find him useful. My last apprentice is .. er .. no longer with me. Tell me, boy, what is your name? Who are your parents?

TOBIAS — My name, sir, is Tobias Stoutheart. My parents, alas sir, are dead.

TODD — (aside) This is good. And tell me, boy, what you would have to offer me as my apprentice?

TOBIAS — I am strong, sir, hard-working, sir, diligent, sir, keen, sir, enthusiastic, intelligent, careful, quick to learn and full of energy, sir.

TODD (aside) Yecchh! I could not stand such a boy. No, boy, I find I do not need an apprentice. (walks away)

TOBIAS And I have money to pay for my education, sir.

(She holds up the banknote. TODD dashes back and grabs it.)

TODD But your story has touched my heart. I will take you on. I happen to have the articles of apprenticeship here.

(He brings out a piece of paper which unfolds to reach from his hand down to the floor and hands TOBIAS a pen.)

Here, sign here. Never mind reading it, just sign.

(TOBIAS signs.)

(aside) Now I have him.

(TODD kicks TOBIAS.)

That is just a sample, boy, of what you will get if you do not do as you are told. You have signed the articles. From now on you will not breathe without my permission. Do you understand?

TOBIAS Yes, Mr Todd.

TODD Yes, Mr Todd, <u>sir</u>.

TOBIAS Yes, Mr Todd, sir.

TODD Now get inside and get to work.

TOBIAS (entering shop) .... and I'm only little.

TODD (to audience) I suppose you feel sorry for the wretch? Do you think <u>kindness</u> is of any use? Would I be where I am today if I had been kind? No! Cruelty is the way and I enjoy it so. But look at the time - and still no customers.

(ALONZO enters DSL carrying an enormous case bearing the words 'THE AMAZING ALONZO'. He puts down the case and looks at the shops.)

Aha! This looks like a likely customer. Well dressed - wealthy perhaps - and a stranger to these parts. I always reserve a warm welcome for strangers. I will prepare something special for him.

(TODD goes into the shop. ALONZO looks back the way he has come on.)

ALONZO (impatiently) Foozle! Oh confound the boy! Foozle!

(FOOZLE enters DSL dressed in ill-fitting and outrageously multi-coloured clothing. He is carrying a dog lead on the end of which is an empty collar.)

FOOZLE Yes, sir. Just coming, sir.

ALONZO (despairingly) Foozle! Oh, how are the mighty fallen! That I, the Amazing Alonzo, illusionist extraordinaire, who have journeyed through the lands of the Arabian nights and mastered all the necromantic arts of the mystic east, should sink so low as to be plagued with an imbecile such as this. (puts his hand to his brow)

FOOZLE (aside) Doesn't he speak lovely?

ALONZO Look boy! Look in your hand. What do you see?

FOOZLE Nothing, sir. (looks more closely) No, I tell a lie it's - uggh! (wipes his hand on his coat)

ALONZO The other hand, simpleton.

FOOZLE (looking at the empty collar) Er?

ALONZO Vacuous villain! Where is Orlando?

FOOZLE Don't worry, sir. He will be close by. I expect he felt like a bit of exercise. A lady dog perhaps, if you know what I mean, sir?

(ALONZO stares coldly at him.)

A lamp-post perhaps. I'll go and find him, sir, shall I? Yes, I shall. Won't take a minute, sir.

ALONZO It is unnecessary, fool. He approaches. Fortunately he is more intelligent than his keeper.

FOOZLE Here, Orlando! Here, boy!

(ORLANDO bounds on, runs around, licks both of them and sits beside ALONZO.)

ALONZO Ah, Orlando! You bring back doleful memories. To think that you and I have enchanted the crowned heads of Europe with our sorcery. Archdukes and kings have begged me to reveal the secrets of my wizardry. An audience. If only there were an audience here I would ....

(FOOZLE looks at the audience.)

...... show you wonders, Foozle.

FOOZLE Well, actually, sir......

ALONZO Miracles I could perform, my boy, but without an audience what purpose would there be?

FOOZLE But look, sir.

(He points to the audience but ALONZO does not look.)

ALONZO Should I waste my incantations upon the empty air? A conjuror without an audience is like a ....

FOOZLE Look, sir.

(ALONZO looks.)

An audience.

(ALONZO steps to the edge of the stage and inspects the audience.)

ALONZO Foolish child! That is not an audience. It is a rabble.

FOOZLE I wouldn't say that, sir.

ALONZO Of course not. You are even more ridiculous than they are, but Orlando knows. I have performed before much greater audiences than this.

(ORLANDO nods in agreement.)

But no, no, you must not beg me to perform an illusion.

(FOOZLE wasn't going to.)

(louder) You must not beg me to perform an illusion..... Well, if you insist. Let me see, what species of illusion would appeal to an audience such as this?

(ORLANDO barks.)

You are right, of course, my faithful hound. My most elementary trick will please their simple minds. Foozle - the receptacle.

FOOZLE Eh?

ALONZO The hat!

(FOOZLE takes a bowler hat out of the case.)

For this illusion I will need the assistance of a member of the audience - you sir, perhaps. Yes, you sir, with the asinine expression. Thank you. Step up here please.

(From the audience VICTIM 1 appears. It is VERY important that the VICTIMS should be cast members.)

Would you hold the receptacle, sir?

(VICTIM 1 takes the hat.)

Foozle, the ingredients.

(FOOZLE produces a jug full of disgusting, sticky goo from the suitcase.)

Thank you. Examine the receptacle, sir. No hidden compartments?

VICTIM 1 — No. (gives hat back)

ALONZO — Observe. (pours the goo into the hat) And now, sir, I am about to test your courage and determination. Close your eyes. I have here a gold sovereign. It is yours, sir. All you have to do is, without opening your eyes, put on the hat.

VICTIM 1 — But ..... (opening eyes)

ALONZO — A gold sovereign, sir. Close your eyes and take the hat.

(ALONZO cleverly substitutes another hat. He can involve ORLANDO in the substitution if desired but it is important that FOOZLE does not see what has happened. VICTIM 1 takes a deep breath and with a quick movement puts on the hat. ALONZO, with a flamboyant gesture approaches him and lifts up the hat. A large amount of confetti falls from inside.)

Voila!

(VICTIM 1 reaches for the gold sovereign but it is pocketed by ALONZO, who is encouraging applause.)

VICTIM 1 — But .... What about .....?

ALONZO — (pushing him back to his seat) A big hand for the gentleman, please.

FOOZLE — That was terrific. Can you do another?

ALONZO — My tricks are wasted on this riff-raff. I am in need of a shave. I will leave Orlando in your charge. Meet me at six o'clock at the Gin Palace in Smithfield. (aside) Yes, to my eternal shame, I have fallen victim to the demon drink. Oh misery! (entering shop) Hello there. I say, fellow! Barber!

FOOZLE — (looking intently at the hat) Yes, I think I see..... Ladies and gentlemen, you are lucky tonight to be present at the first performance of the Great Foozle! I need a volunteer from the audience. Ah, the very man!

(VICTIM 2 is brought on stage from audience.)

Thank you, sir. You saw this trick just now.

VICTIM 2 — I did.

FOOZLE — Right then. Cop hold of that. (hands him hat) Oh, sorry. (takes hat back and imitates ALONZO's tone) Would you please examine the receptacle .... and now the ingredients. (pours more goo into hat) And now if you will take the receptacle, please sir. I am about to test your courage, your determination. Close your eyes, sir.

(VICTIM 2 does so eagerly.)

If you can now put on the hat, I have here .... I have here ..... (searches his pockets) I have here half a bacon sandwich. It could be yours. Courage, sir. Put on the hat.

(Before VICTIM 2 can do so, ALONZO comes out of the shop.)

ALONZO — Foozle! What are you doing to this poor old gentleman? I'm so sorry, sir. Please excuse my assistant. Very sorry.....

(He guides VICTIM 2 back to his seat.)

I will deal with the boy severely, I assure you.

(FOOZLE sneaks off.)

Where has he gone? And confound this barber! There is not a sign of the man. Orlando! Has he left you here alone? That boy suffers from terminal incompetence. Wait there, Orlando. I will try once more to arouse this barber.

(He turns and bumps into TODD in the doorway.)

TODD Forgive me, sir. I have been detained. Certain preparations were necessary for a satisfactory - er - execution on your throat.

ALONZO Indeed, sir, I become daily more accustomed to feckless inefficiency.

TODD Thank you, sir. Step inside please. I will be with you in one moment.

(ALONZO enters shop.)

'Certain preparations.' Ha ha haaaaa! His clothes suggest that he is worth a sovereign or two. His suit alone will fetch a guinea. Ha ha haaaa! Oh, sometimes I'm so rotten I can't stand it. Ha ha!

(ORLANDO growls.)

What's that? Get away from here you flea-bitten mutt. Get away, I say!

(He kicks ORLANDO who cringes and howls. As TODD turns away ORLANDO attacks him from behind. There is an enormous fight but ORLANDO is chased off.)

If there are two things I hate - animals ..... and people. You know sometimes I look in the mirror and I say, 'Sweeney, how did you ever become so deliciously evil?' Evil. I love the sound of the word. Evil! Evil! Evil!!! Ha ha haaaaaaaa!

(Green lights come up as MUSIC 3 begins.)

<u>I'm Evil!</u>

I'm evil.
I'm wicked. I enjoy it.
I'm evil.
All virtue I'll destroy it.

There's not a shop in London town
(Throughout the trade it's known),
Can polish off a customer
As quickly as my own!

I'm evil.
My wit is razor sharp.
I'm evil.
Soon he'll be playing on a harp.

I'm evil.
You really have to laugh.
My razor
Will saw this conjuror in half.

There's not a shop in London town
(Throughout the trade it's known),
Can polish off a customer
As quickly as my own!

It's shocking
How much I cherish sin.
He's waiting
Now I shall go and do him in!

(TODD is about to go into a spectacular dance but is interrupted by shouts from offstage.)

ANGELO (off) Signore! Signore! (rushes on in an agitated state) Signore! Signore!

(TODD ignores him.)

Signore! Signore!

(ANGELO tugs TODD's sleeve.)

TODD — Take your macaroni-stained fingers off my coat! What is it you want?

ANGELO — Signore Todd. My mistress, Signora Lovett, she wisha you piss.

TODD — (giving him a look) Peace. She wishes me peace. You mangle the English language with your Neapolitan nonsense. What is it you want?

ANGELO — Oh, Signore Todd. Angelo - is a me - have a da important message from Signora Lovett. Is a very important.

TODD — Well?

ANGELO — Is a very important.

TODD — I know 'is a very important', but WHAT IS IT?

ANGELO — I forget.

(TODD raises his fist.)

I remember.

(MRS LOVETT enters USL behind ANGELO.)

TODD — Well?

ANGELO — She tella me .... she tella me ....

(He catches sight of MRS LOVETT and is thrown into a panic.)

Ah, Signora Lovett ... I remember .... I remember

(MRS LOVETT approaches threateningly.)

You say .... no wait ... I remember .... Don't hit me ..... Signora .... per favore ... aiuto ... ohh!

(ANGELO is now sandwiched tightly between TODD and MRS LOVETT. He sinks to his knees. MRS LOVETT takes hold of one ear and gestures towards the other.)

MRS LOVETT Mr Todd?

(TODD takes the other ear and they lift ANGELO to his feet.)

I have a kind heart, Mr Todd.

TODD Indeed, Mrs Lovett.

MRS LOVETT I have been like a mother to this boy, Mr Todd.

TODD I have often thought so, Mrs Lovett.

MRS LOVETT He is Italian you know, Mr Todd.

TODD I had an inkling, Mrs Lovett.

MRS LOVETT It was my kind heart that led me to take him in. He was penniless, starving. He had stowed away in a ship bound for London. When he arrived here he knew not a word of the language. I found him lying in the gutter not fifty yards from this very spot. Who knows what might have become of him if I had not taken him in?

(ANGELO is standing on tiptoe, his ears still firmly held by TODD and MRS LOVETT.)

TODD Who indeed?

MRS LOVETT And yet despite my kindness, my generosity, my .. ... er ...

TODD Your magnanimity?

MRS LOVETT The very word ... my mahogany. Despite all this the boy is ungrateful.

TODD Surely not.

MRS LOVETT Sadly yes.

ANGELO Plis signora....

MRS LOVETT He is workshy.

ANGELO No signora.

MRS LOVETT Si signora. If you will excuse me, Mr Todd.

(TODD releases his ear. MRS LOVETT leads ANGELO to the edge of the stage and kicks him back to her shop.)

Back to the bakehouse. See to the ovens. The latest batch of my delicious pies should be nearly ready. Speaking of the shop, Mr Todd.....

(She makes sure ANGELO has gone into shop.)

I find myself a little short of ... er ... pie filling, Mr Todd.

(Nudge, nudge, wink, wink.)

TODD Why do you not speak to the butcher, Mrs Lovett.

MRS LOVETT (aside) The barbarous villain plays games with me! No butcher can supply me with meat of the quality my customers have come to expect.

TODD Your customers. Ah yes. Indeed, I see a bigger throng about your door each day. Your business is expanding and to think that I can remember when you first went into the pie business. You were finding it difficult to make both ends meet (meat). (aside) I will make her sweat.

MRS LOVETT (aside) He tries my patience. You know my meaning!

TODD Now understand my meaning. I have a fresh supply of meat. (gestures to his shop door)

MRS LOVETT How fresh?

TODD — Not yet slaughtered. But there has been a slight increase in my prices. Inflation, you know.

MRS LOVETT — How much?

TODD — Double.

MRS LOVETT — You ... you ... Sir, we had an agreement!

TODD — (aside) We never meet but like gunpowder and fire there is an explosion!

MRS LOVETT — I have been a fool to fall in with your murderous schemes. Yet what can I do? Without your 'meat' my pie shop would be ruined. My customers are mad for my 'veal' pies. They worship my gravy. If only they knew what they were eating. I have no alternative, Mr Todd. I will pay your price.

TODD — There is money for both of us in this, my friend. (aside) She is no friend of mine! (together)

MRS LOVETT — (aside) He is no friend of mine! (together)

TODD — If my share is greater than yours, it is because my part of the work is more hazardous.

MRS LOVETT — Spare me your fatuous explanations, Mr Todd. You force me against my will to perform all manner of evils.

TODD — Force you, Mrs Lovett? Come now, confess. Do you not feel the slightest satisfaction in your work?

MRS LOVETT — What an idea!

TODD — Be truthful. Is there not a tingle of pleasure that comes with each evil deed?

MRS LOVETT — Well, er ....

TODD — Yes?

MRS LOVETT — YES! I do enjoy it! Why should I pretend otherwise? Sometimes I look at myself in the mirror and I say,

'Wilhemina Lovett, how did you ever become so magnificently wicked?'

(Lights dim, they cackle. MUSIC 4 starts.)

We're Evil!

TODD & MRS LOVETT

We're evil!
We're nasty and we're mean.
We're evil!
We make a gruesome team.

There's not a shop in London town
(It's not within their powers)
Can bake or sell a hot meat pie
With gravy such as ours.

We're rotten
We murder and we steal.
We butcher!
In the pies we call it veal!

We're nasty.
Murdered corpses by the ton.
It's ghastly,
But we have a lot of fun!

There's not a shop in London town
(It's not within their powers)
Can bake or sell a hot meat pie -
If they knew the truth we bet they'd die.
Can bake or sell a hot meat pie -
We think you know the reason why.
Can bake or sell a hot meat pie
With a gravy such as ours!

I'm evil!
S/he's evil!
We're evil!

(Exeunt with a final horrifying cackle. MRS LOVETT to her shop and TODD to his. As they go two sailors enter DSL. BILLY is young and handsome, TOMMY is older with a thick beard and a parrot on his shoulder.)

TOMMY What do you think of London, Billy, on your first visit? Wonderful, isn't it?

BILLY 'Wonderful' I expect that's the word for it, Tommy.

TOMMY You'll enjoy it, Billy. With all the wealth we have after our voyage you'll find you're a very popular character in this fair city. I will show you all the sights, starting with the gin palace of my old friend, Beaujolais Pickle, where we will find sweet liquor and good company. Let's waste no more time, I'm developing a thirst.

BILLY I am not a drinking man, shipmate, as you know, but I will join you for an hour for friendship's sake, and then I must journey on. To think that in a few short hours I shall see again the face of my beloved Susan.

TOMMY She must be a rare sweetheart for your passion to survive a voyage of such length.

(During the following speech the sounds of seagulls, waves, ship's rigging and stirring nautical music are heard, slowly increasing in volume.)

BILLY I have been three years at sea and in all that time I have heard but once from Susan. She has been a mainstay to me in all weathers. I have been roused from my hammock, dreaming of her, for the cold, black, middle watch. I have walked the deck, the spray beating in my face, but Susan was at my side and I did not feel it. I have been reefing on the yards in cold and darkness, when I could hardly see the hand of my next messmate but Susan's eyes were on me and there was light. When 'land' was cried from the masthead I seized the glass. My shipmates saw the cliffs of England - I, I could see but Susan. I leapt upon the dock, my shipmates find hands to grasp and lips to press - I find not Susan's...... (by now he is shouting to be heard over the sound effects).... But tomorrow as the dawn kisses the fields of Kent, I shall kiss the lips of the fairest flower in England - my Susan. (sound effects end abruptly)

TOMMY (waking from a daydream) Sorry. What did you say?

(Sound effects begin again.)

BILLY I have been three years at sea ....

TOMMY (cutting across, sound effects stop) We're wasting good drinking time, shipmate. Come - to the gin palace.

BILLY I will join you shortly but first I must buy for my dearest Susan the gift that I have promised her on my return.

TOMMY A gift?

BILLY I promised to place round her exquisite throat a string of pearls which would match the beauty of her fair skin.

TOMMY A string of pearls?

BILLY Sometimes I wonder if I'm talking to you or the parrot. Yes, a string of pearls. Look, I have ....

(ANGELO enters USL from Pie Shop and sees the sailors. He is full of admiration.)

...... copied these lines from a book of poetry.
'The hours I spent with thee, dear heart,
Are as a string of pearls to me.
I count them over every one apart,
My rosary.'

ANGELO (aside) Ah sailors! How I woulda love to joina da navy. I sail to here from Italy and all I see isa da inside ofa da lifeboat, but now I wish to see da beauties of da world. Bellissima ....

(TOMMY and BILLY come over to him.)

...... to have a signorina ina every port.

BILLY — You are right, lad. A good uniform works its way with the women.

TOMMY — It's a grand life in the navy.

ANGELO — Will you tell me, signore, of your life in the navy?

TOMMY — Sing the lad your song, Billy.

BILLY — Stow it, Tommy. I am no singer.

TOMMY — No singer! Bless you, lad. Whenever we want to catch a mermaid, we only make Billy sing a verse and we've twenty round the ship. Less of your modesty. Sing for the lad.

BILLY — Oh, very well, but you'll have to help me out.

MUSIC 5 We Love the Navy

BILLY & TOMMY

When we were lads sitting on our mothers' knees
We dreamed of a life sailing on the seven seas.
Now that we're grown we have sailed the whole world wide,
From Liverpool to Hong Kong, from Wapping to Port Said.

We love the Nav-ee,
The swell of the sea.
Travelling free,
We run with the tide,
We sail side by side,
The stars are our guide.

TOMMY

If you're small or sickly, if people pick on you,
Sign on for naval training. You'll find what they say is true,
Soon you'll have muscles strong as iron, nerves like steel and suntanned skin.
They'll be no girl that you can't charm, no fight that you can't win.

BILLY & TOMMY

We love the Nav-ee,
The swell of the sea.

Travelling free,
We run with the tide,
We sail side by side,
The stars are our guide.

BILLY

If you're a lad who is keen to see the world,
Then hoist up your anchor, let your mainsail be unfurled.
Cast off and set a course to find horizons new,
To see wonders that lie hidden from all but a chosen few.

BILLY & TOMMY & ANGELO

We love the Nav-ee,
The swell of the sea.
Travelling free,
We run with the tide,
We sail side by side,
The stars are our guide.

(They have been performing a complicated dance involving all the traditional sailors' duties - hauling ropes, climbing the mast, keeping a lookout etc. During the last chorus ANGELO attempts to join in causing them to become entangled with each other. All three exit DSR repeating chorus as they go. The lights dim and a large notice is carried across the stage - 'MEANWHILE'.)

Scene 2 Inside TODD's shop

(ALONZO is sitting in the chair USC. TOBIAS is mixing the shaving soap. TODD is sharpening his razor. Some levers are on the wall USR, door USL.)

ALONZO

Devil take you, sir. You are the slowest barber it has ever been my misfortune to meet.

TODD

Nay, sir. I will very soon polish you off. Ha haaa!

(His laugh is so loud and horrifying that TOBIAS drops the bowl of shaving soap.)

Give me that. You shall pay later for your clumsiness.

ALONZO Come, sir. My beard has grown another inch while I have sat here in the chair.

TODD Coming, sir, coming. Tobias, step around the corner and find the time on St Dunstan's church clock while I finish this gentleman off.

TOBIAS It is ten o'clock, sir. I have just heard it strike.

TODD Oh .... well, Tobias, run along to Mr Woolworth's store and collect the razor I left there to be sharpened.

TOBIAS It is here, sir. He brought it himself not ten minutes since.

TODD Very well, Tobias. Go to Mistress Tesco's modern emporium and purchase a dozen of her delicious muffins.

TOBIAS But, Mr Todd, there are two plates of muffins in the parlour. You cannot require more.

TODD TOBIAS! Never mind the time, disregard the razor, abandon the muffins, but GO, DEPART, RETIRE, WITHDRAW, TAKE YOUR LEAVE, MAKE TRACKS ......

(Hitting TOBIAS with every word.)

...... SLING YOUR HOOK!

TOBIAS I think I'll go now, if you don't mind. (aside as she leaves) This is strange behaviour. And it's not fair - I'm only little.

TODD Now, sir, your shave.

ALONZO Never in my considerable experience of establishments throughout the length and breadth of Europe, nay the world, have I had the misfortune to meet a barber of such monumental incompetence, such ....

(TODD gives him a mouthful of soap.)

TODD That has stopped your mouth, sir, and now I shall stop it permanently.

(With a grand gesture he slits ALONZO's throat laughing madly.)

But there is no time to waste. I must dispose of the evidence. The lever.

(He goes to the levers on the wall USR and pulls one. The lights go out.)

Wrong lever!

(Lights come on again and he selects a second lever. The chair disappears through the wall. There is a long falling sound and a thud. TODD laughs madly.)

Now to see what this ill-tempered conjuror was worth.

(He exits USL and the chair returns to its original position as TOBIAS enters DSL from street.)

TOBIAS (going over to the chair and kneeling down to inspect the trap/secret door) This is curious. What is the purpose of this trap-door?

(TODD enters USL with a pile of clothes, sees TOBIAS and throws the clothes back through the doorway. Creeps up on TOBIAS from behind.)

TODD What are you doing, boy?

TOBIAS (leaping up) Nothing, Mr Todd.

TODD Why were you kneeling on the floor?

TOBIAS I .. er .. just tripped, Mr Todd.

TODD Tripped? (aside) Does he suspect?

(He grabs TOBIAS threateningly.)

Be warned my inquisitive young friend. It would be most unwise, most unwise, for you to repeat a word of what passes in this shop, or dare to make any supposition or draw any conclusion from anything you see or hear, or fancy you see or hear. Do you understand me? Eh? Eh?

TOBIAS (terrified) Yes, sir. I won't say anything, sir.

(TODD moves away.)

If I as much as say one word, sir, I wish I may be made into veal pies at Mrs Lovett's next door, sir.

(TODD freezes in his tracks.)

TODD How dare you mention veal pies in my presence! (aside) I think I shall have to polish the boy off.

(TODD is about to kill TOBIAS then and there when the street door opens DSL and ORLANDO bursts in. He runs around and barks madly at the chair. TODD tries to kick him and falls over.)

Tobias! Don't just stand there. Catch hold of the pestilential animal.

(TOBIAS does so.)

Now take him to the river - and throw him in!

(ORLANDO howls.)

With a stone tied around his neck!

TOBIAS But sir ....

TODD Do as I say!

TOBIAS Yes, sir.

(Exit DSL dragging ORLANDO with him.)

TODD Cursed animal. And the magician, for all his fine

words had precious little of value on his person. Perhaps his clothing will fetch a price. (picks up clothes from doorway USL) Let me see. This cloak is of good quality and the shirt is of fine material,too, but what is this? Curse you,Sweeney Todd, for a clumsy fool! Blood! Here - and there. Damnation! I dare not let these be seen. They are fit only for the furnace. No money! Worthless clothing! This magician has played a last trick even in death. Yet his body will, I am sure, be of use to my grisly pie-maker neighbour. I should meet no problems with that sale. But Sweeney, you must learn from this mistake. Trust in the chair, Sweeney. Ay, the chair. Why slit throats and spill blood when a long fall and a broken neck will do the job with less sanguification?

(BILLY enters from street door DSL. TODD quickly hides the clothing.)

Good morning, sir. Can I help you?

BILLY Good morrow, friend. I have need of your craft. Let my hair be cut at once for tomorrow I have to meet a lady.

TODD You have come then to the right establishment. The finest barber shop in the city,sir. Please sit down. You're not a Londoner yourself, sir?

BILLY No, I return to the village of my birth tonight.

TODD You have been at sea, sir?

BILLY Yes. I have only lately come up the river from an Indian voyage.

TODD A great distance, sir.

(TODD steps back in amazement as he notices the string of pearls in BILLY's pocket. He walks forward and addresses the audience.)

I can scarcely believe my eyes. Can it be a string of pearls that hangs from his pocket? (going back)

Pardon me, sir, but can that be a string of pearls that hangs from your pocket?

BILLY — What? Oh yes, indeed. I am glad you spoke of it. In confidence let me tell you, they are of the value of twelve thousand pounds. I must be more careful.

TODD — Yes, there are some wicked people in this city. You would hardly believe how wicked. But sit back, sir, and relax. Close your eyes. It will all be over before you know what has happened.

(BILLY sits in the chair and shuts his eyes. TODD goes USR and pulls the lever. BILLY screams as he disappears.)

This is better. A string of pearls and a fine new naval uniform. I must let Mrs Lovett know that I have <u>two</u> carcases for her attention. I must see to the body.

(Exit TODD USL. TOBIAS enters from the street DSL with a POLICE CONSTABLE.)

TOBIAS — (entering) My master does not seem to be here at present, sir. I will tell him you wish to speak with him.

CONSTABLE — Don't trouble yourself young man. I will await his return.

(The CONSTABLE wanders round inspecting the shop.)

TOBIAS — (aside) To lie is a wicked thing but I must lie to my master. I could not bring myself to drown the dog. I set him free in the park. He will not trouble my master further.

(TODD returns carrying the pearls and the sailor's uniform. He doesn't notice the CONSTABLE and TOBIAS. He holds up the uniform.)

TODD — (pleased) Not a stain.

CONSTABLE Mr Todd?

(TODD jumps in the air with fright. He throws the clothes on to the table by the door. TOBIAS goes USL to inspect them.)

TODD Yes ... er ... I am Sweeney Todd.

CONSTABLE (taking out his notebook) I would like a word with you.

TODD Er ... yes?

(TOBIAS holds up the uniform.)

TOBIAS He is dead, sir.

(TODD turns in terror.)

TODD What? NO! What do you mean?

TOBIAS (surprised) The dog, sir. You instructed me to kill him. He is dead, sir.

TODD Ah, the dog! Of course, the dog, yes. He is dead. (to CONSTABLE) The dog. Dead. The dog - dead.

CONSTABLE Yes, sir. As I understand it the dog is dead, sir?

TODD Yes.

(He snatches the clothing from TOBIAS and throws it through doorway USL.)

You wanted to speak to me?

CONSTABLE Yes, Mr Todd. On the subject of theft, Mr Todd ....

(TODD finds he still has the pearls in his hand and stiffens, bundling them out of sight.)

... and murder, Mr Todd.

TODD (picking up razor) Theft? MURDER!?

CONSTABLE As I was passing down the street, in a southerly direction, at fifteen minutes past midnight, this very morning, Mr Todd....

TODD Yes? (aside) What has he seen? My heart misgives.

CONSTABLE Your front door was unlocked. You could have been robbed, Mr Todd. You could have been murdered in your bed.

TODD Oh! Oh, I see. Well, thank you, constable. I will be more careful in future. Thank you very much.

(He pushes CONSTABLE to the door.)

CONSTABLE (as he leaves) Theft, Mr Todd. Murder, Mr Todd.

TODD (to TOBIAS) Murder, Mr Todd. Murder, Mr Todd! I will murder you, bringing a policeman in here. What do you mean by it?

TOBIAS Mean, Mr Todd?

TODD Yes, very mean! I am famous for it! You shall see how mean I can be!

(He approaches TOBIAS threateningly.)

TOBIAS (aside) It's not fair this, you know. I'll be black and blue by the interval - and I'm only little!

(TODD and TOBIAS move to opposite sides of the stage as MUSIC 6 begins.)

I'm Only Little

TOBIAS

When I first came here I had my doubts.
I cannot please him, he screams and shouts.
He kicks and beats me and more besides,
I'm only little - but it hurts my pride!

I'm only thirteen but every day
My skin is ageing, hair turning grey.
I'm poor, I'm lonely, nowhere to hide,
I'm only little - no one's on my side!

I thought he'd help me, my life he'd save.
I signed a paper - became a slave -
But was he honest? Now you decide,
I'm only little and I could have cried!

TODD

I'll have to kill him
he stirs my bile.
It aggravates me
to see him smile.
It won't look like murder
but suicide.
He's only little -
but troublesome besides.

TODD & TOBIAS together

This irritating creature has no respect. And the secrets of my business he may detect If he ever knows he will certainly expose me. I see it in my nightmares Does he suspect?	But this must end soon I have it planned. For I'll not take it - I'll make a stand. My sense of duty shall be my guide, I'm only little - but I'm big inside!
I'll have to kill him he stirs my bile. It aggravates me to see him smile. It won't look like murder but suicide. He's only little - but troublesome besides.	Mournful sighs, plaintive cries. Are my senses telling lies? Fearful moans, Hopeless groans, Creeping from the cellar stones.
This irritating creature - Does he suspect?	I'm only little - But I'm big inside

(TODD begins to beat TOBIAS but is interrupted by MRS LOVETT entering DSL.)

TODD Get out, boy! GET OUT! (pushes him off DSR)

MRS LOVETT Mr Todd, I have been insulted.

TODD That Italian brat up to his tricks again?

MRS LOVETT No. I have locked <u>him</u> in the bakehouse. I fear he may begin to understand the evil nature of the work he performs. I shall keep him in future under lock and key.

TODD How then have you been insulted?

MRS LOVETT Through Her Majesty's Post Office, Mr Todd. (waves letter in the air) They have insulted me. They have dared to ask for my rent.

TODD No!

MRS LOVETT They have. They demand £40, Mr Todd.

TODD £40! How long is it since you paid?

MRS LOVETT Well .... let me see .... not long .... er ... three, four .... no, it must be five .... yes ... five years.

TODD Ha ha haaaa! So they have finally caught up with you!

MRS LOVETT I'm glad you're amused, Mr Todd, as it is you who will have to pay.

(TODD chokes.)

Be sure if I am arrested for debt, Mr Todd, there may be others who will be as sorry as I. Do you understand me?

TODD You dare to demand money from me? (aside) I see she too will have to be polished off.

HECKLER Ah shut up!

(The HECKLER should be in the balcony if there is one or at the back of the audience. If there is a balcony two seats will need to be occupied by the HECKLER and the dummy. HECKLER stands.)

TODD Who said that?

HECKLER I did, up here. You're rubbish. Get off.

TODD (shading his eyes) Who is it? Brian Clough?

MRS LOVETT It could be the drama critic from the (local paper).

HECKLER Let's see somebody who can act. Bring the dog back on.

MRS LOVETT (to TODD) Keep him talking. (runs off stage)

HECKLER That's right. Come back when you're sober.

TODD Everybody has the right to be stupid, sir, but you abuse the privilege.

HECKLER I don't know which is worse, your acting or your singing. As for him playing the piano - as a pianist he'd make a good ratcatcher.

TODD Now listen, my man, these people have paid good money to come in here tonight.

HECKLER How much do they have to pay to get out?

(This can continue with references to local events and personalities for as long as is necessary for MRS LOVETT to make her way to the balcony or the back of the audience. She dashes in shouting:)

MRS LOVETT Right you! Out! Come on!

HECKLER Who's going to make me?

(There is a furious fight. The HECKLER is finally vanquished and either thrown over the balcony - the dummy having been cunningly substituted - or if there is no balcony, MRS LOVETT pushes her way through the audience, drags out the HECKLER , hits him on the head and throws him to the floor.)

MRS LOVETT (shouting to TODD) That's dealt with the rowdy element. What do you think?

TODD Veal and ham by the look of him.

MRS LOVETT How about my money, Mr Todd?

TODD We will discuss it later. I will meet you this evening at the gin palace of Beaujolais Pickle.

(MRS LOVETT leaves. The 'body' is removed. TODD holds up the pearls in a spotlight DSC.)

When a boy, the thirst of avarice was first awakened by the fair gift of a farthing; that farthing soon became a pound; the pound a hundred, so to a thousand, till I said to myself, I will possess a hundred thousand. This string of pearls will complete the sum. Ha ha haaaaaa!

(The curtains close on TODD's demoniacal laughter. FOOZLE enters in front of curtains carrying case.)

FOOZLE (looking left and right) Ah, excuse me, sir. This looks like a good opportunity..... If you would return to the stage, sir.

(VICTIM 2 does so, and FOOZLE takes the hat and jug out of the case to repeat trick but,just as the VICTIM 2 is about to put on the hat he is tapped on the shoulder by the POLICE CONSTABLE.)

CONSTABLE 'ello, 'ello, 'ello. What's goin' on 'ere then?

FOOZLE Just a little trick, officer.

CONSTABLE (taking hat from VICTIM 2) Do you have a licence as a street performer?

FOOZLE Well ... er .... no.

CONSTABLE Well, I shall have to ask you to move along,please. Come along, don't dawdle. And you, sir, please. (peering closely at VICTIM 2) Haven't I seen you on one of my wanted posters? You're not the Finsbury Flasher, are you? No? Well, move along then please. I'm sure I've seen him somewhere.

(As FOOZLE, the CONSTABLE and VICTIM 2 leave the stage the curtains open for the next scene.)

Scene 3 PICKLE's Gin Palace

(The scene is one of great activity and noise. The stage is set with a great many tables and stools, the bar is USR with a door to the street USL. Most of the CUSTOMERS are well on the way to passing out. CHILDREN sit on the floor drinking what they can steal from the tables. BEAUJOLAIS PICKLE, the proprietor is rushing about from table to table with large jugs labelled 'GIN'. He is assisted by GROVEL,his waiter. There are two 'special' tables at opposite sides of the stage DSR and DSL. TOMMY is sitting at the DSR one.)

CUSTOMER 1 Pickle! Pickle! Where is the man? Pickle!

PICKLE Yes, sir. Coming, sir. More gin, sir?

CUSTOMER 1 No! I will have wine. There is some demon in my heart that leaps at the sound of the word. The monster's up and wine, wine alone, can satisfy it.

PICKLE Grovel! Come here at once, Grovel.

(GROVEL dashes over.)

GROVEL Yes, sir.

PICKLE Grovel, wine for this customer.

GROVEL (throwing back his head) Owoooooooooo!

(CUSTOMER 2 staggers to the centre.)

CUSTOMER 2 Gentlemen .... and ladies, a toast. The Queen!

(All the CUSTOMERS stand and raise their glasses.)

CUSTOMERS The Queen! (drink and sit in perfect unison)

CUSTOMER 2 Oh what a perfect world would this be if all the green fields were tobacco and all the rivers gin! (coughs disgustingly and staggers back to his seat)

PICKLE — Indeed, sir. It is a most refreshing liquor. How would we manage without it in these sad and troubled times? It strengthens the spirit, improves the health, broadens the mind .....

(CUSTOMER 3 leaps to her feet.)

CUSTOMER 3 — LADIES and gentlemen! The Queen!

CUSTOMERS — (rising as before) The Queen! (drink and sit in perfect unison)

CUSTOMER 4 — (struggling to his feet) The QUEEN! (falls flat on his face and is ignored by everyone except the CHILDREN who go through his pockets)

TOMMY — I wonder what has become of my shipmate. It is late. He should have met me long since. He would not fail. I hope he has not met with some accident.

CUSTOMER 1 — Come, let's have a song!

CUSTOMER 3 — (who fancies herself a bit of a prima donna)Mr Pickle, we will sing the praises of your entrancing, enrapturing and enchanting liquor. Let us sing, ladies and gentlemen - to gin!

CUSTOMERS — (rising) To gin!

MUSIC 7 Gin!

PICKLE — If your breath is short or if your eyes are dim -
CUSTOMERS — drink gin!
PICKLE — If exhausted or weak in the head or limb -
CUSTOMERS — try gin!

GROVEL — Don't believe them when they tell you it's a sin -
CUSTOMERS — not gin!
GROVEL — If you feel temptation, don't resist, give in -
CUSTOMERS — to gin!

ALL — Gin! Gin!
We'll always love it right or wrong.
Gin! Gin!

The inspiration for our song.
Gin! Gin!
Your servants we will always be.
Gin! Gin!
A kind of liquid poetry!

BOY 1 — It makes no difference how young you begin -
CUSTOMERS — with gin.
GIRL 1 — It's a friend who'll stick with you through thick & thin
CUSTOMERS — is gin!

CUSTOMER 1 — You can drink it if you're fat or if you're thin -
ALL — good gin.
CUSTOMER 1 — It will bring a healthy glow to every skin -
ALL — will gin!

ALL — CHORUS

CUSTOMER 2 — It's on sale in every pub and bar and inn -
ALL — fine gin.
CUSTOMER 2 — It's the reason for old Gilbert's foolish grin -
ALL — is gin!

CUSTOMER 3 — Drink it from a glass, a bucket or a bin -
ALL — drink gin.
CUSTOMER 3 — Tell the waiter to fill right up to the brim -
ALL — with gin.

ALL — CHORUS

CUSTOMER 5 — If you choose it you can bet you'll always win -
ALL — on gin.
CUSTOMER 5 — Your eyes will blur, your knees go weak, your head will spin -
ALL — with gin!

(CUSTOMER 5 is very drunk and staggers about unable to carry on with the next two lines. There is a moment of confusion as he is helped to a seat then everyone launches into the chorus:)

ALL — Gin! Gin!
We'll always love it right or wrong.
Gin! Gin!

The inspiration for our song.
Gin! Gin!
Your servants we will always be.
GIN! GIN!
A KIND OF LIQUID POETRY!

(As the song ends there is a total collapse on the floor and GILBERT who has not taken part in the song comes forward to the centre. He is at least two hundred years old, bent double and using a stick.)

GILBERT Waha! Weedolberingle. Gerasticleecontertiblust.

(He laughs eccentrically - it is not necessary for GILBERT to stick too rigidly to the script!)

CUSTOMER 1 (rising from floor) Yes, yes, Gilbert. Ha ha!

(CUSTOMERS all look at each other mystified. They all climb back to their seats. GILBERT sits with great difficulty at the table with TOMMY. FOOZLE enters USL carrying case with ORLANDO following.)

FOOZLE At last. It's taken me hours to find this place. It is almost six o'clock now. The Amazing Alonzo should be here soon. (sees ORLANDO) Orlando! I thought you had stayed with my master.

(ORLANDO nods.)

You did? Is he here then?

(ORLANDO shakes his head.)

Where is he then?

(ORLANDO runs to the door USL and comes back.)

What do you mean?

(ORLANDO takes FOOZLE's coat tails in his mouth and pulls.)

Stop it! I'm not going anywhere. It's cold out there

and in here it's warm and comfortable. (looks around) Well, it's warm anyway. (sits at table DSL)

(ORLANDO whimpers mournfully.)

Waiter, bring me something to warm me on this chill night.

GROVEL Gin? Brandy? Rum? Wine? Champagne?

FOOZLE Er .....

GROVEL Claret? Port? Whisky? Stout?

FOOZLE Have you got any cocoa?

GROVEL One mug of cocoa, sir. Yes, sir. Anything else?

FOOZLE Yes, the dog could do with a drink, too.

GROVEL Yes, sir.

CUSTOMER 1 Gentlemen! The Queen!

CUSTOMERS (rising) THE QUEEN! (sit in unison)

(GROVEL brings drinks for FOOZLE and ORLANDO.)

FOOZLE (tasting drink) What game are you playing? This is water. (throws it at GROVEL)

GROVEL I beg your pardon, sir.

(GROVEL takes the dog dish from ORLANDO and pours the contents into FOOZLE's mug.)

GILBERT (to TOMMY) Gureegooberindipolikgingle, atakabol.

(CUSTOMERS 1 and 3 gather round as he speaks.)

CUSTOMER 1 Oh aye, Gilbert.

CUSTOMER 3 Always one for a jest, eh Gilbert?

TOMMY — Er .... excuse me ... what did he say?

CUSTOMER 3 — Oh bless you, sir. No one has understood a word Gilbert has said for the past fifteen years.

GILBERT — Gabble, babble, gabble. (laughs uproariously, the others join in)

CUSTOMER 2 — (rising) Ladies and gentlemen! The Queen!

CUSTOMERS — (rising) THE QUEEN!

(GILBERT has joined in and as everybody sits in unison so he falls over. He is carried out, still bent double, legs in the air.)

CUSTOMER 1 — Come on, Gilbert. Time you were in bed. Give us a hand with him, Charlie.

(CUSTOMERS 1 and 5 bump into TODD in the entrance USL as they carry GILBERT out.)

TODD — Out of my way, ruffians!

PICKLE — Welcome, Mr Todd.

TODD — (ignoring him) Waiter! Bring me wine! Quickly fool!

(He walks over to TOMMY's table DSR, points over TOMMY's head. TOMMY turns round. From under his coat TODD produces a 'RESERVED' sign which he places on the table.)

Excuse me, I think you are sitting at my table. If you wouldn't mind.....

(TOMMY is puzzled but leaves and crosses to table DSL where FOOZLE is sitting.)

I see my mutinous partner in crime is late once again. I become more and more impatient with her snivelling cowardice but,more important - she is becoming a danger to me. I shall have to make plans for her disposal.

CUSTOMER 3 (rising) Ladies and gentlemen! The Queen!

CUSTOMERS (rising) THE QUEEN!

(They all sit in unison having toasted, including TODD who is very patriotic. TOMMY returns to the table DSR.)

TOMMY Excuse me. It is Mr Todd, I believe. Mr Sweeney Todd, the barber?

TODD Indeed that is my name and trade. What business have you with me?

TOMMY It is late. Your shop is closed?

TODD No, I'm there now shaving a customer. Of course it is closed!

TOMMY This is curious, sir. My shipmate, Billy, was to meet me here as soon as you had dealt with him.

TODD (standing and addressing audience) Dealt with him? Indeed I have dealt with him. Ha ha haaaaaaa! (returning to TOMMY and sitting) I know nothing of your friend, sir. I have shaved no sailors today. Do not bother me. (turns away)

TOMMY (going DSL) You are most uncivil, sir. Good evening to you. (aside) Something seems to whisper in my ear that this fellow knows of my friend's fate.

CUSTOMER 2 (rising) Gentlemen! The Queen!

CUSTOMERS (rising) THE QUEEN! (all sit in unison)

(FOOZLE crosses to TODD, ORLANDO follows.)

FOOZLE Mr Sweeney Todd, I believe?

TODD I have that honour.

FOOZLE My master, the Amazing Alonzo ... (points to name on the case, TODD starts) ... visited your shop this afternoon. He arranged to meet me here at six. I wonder if he gave you any idea as to his plans after he left your shop?

TODD (stepping over to audience) Left my shop? Little does the poor fool know his master never left my shop. Ha ha haaaaaa!

(As he returns to the table ORLANDO snaps at him.)

Curse this confounded dog! It plagues me.

FOOZLE You know the dog?

TODD (quickly) Know it? How should I know it? What do you mean? Be gone! You weary me! (aside) That cursed boy Tobias has disobeyed me once too often!

FOOZLE (returning to table DSL) I will not stay where I am not welcome. (aside) This behaviour is most suspicious!

(MRS LOVETT enters and joins TODD at table DSR.)

TOMMY (to FOOZLE) I noticed that you were speaking to Mr Sweeney Todd.

FOOZLE Yes, indeed. You know, it is most curious ......

(Their conversation becomes inaudible and interspersed with that of TODD and MRS LOVETT.)

MRS LOVETT Perhaps I find you in a better humour in the company of your thieving companion here?

(TODD looks around.)

(tapping the bottle) This gentleman here. He robs people of their brains, their digestion and their conscience - to say nothing of their money. Speaking of which, Mr Todd, as I told you earlier I am in urgent need of £40.

TODD Ah, yes, the £40.

MRS LOVETT (aside) If I ply him with drink, I may get it out of him..... Allow me to fill your glass, Mr Todd.

TOMMY (to FOOZLE) You amaze me, sir. My situation is almost identical. My companion ....

MRS LOVETT (to TODD) I have some inkling, Mr Todd, of the wealth you have acquired through your evil trade. £40 is nothing to a man of your means. Come sir!

TODD Say no more, Mrs Lovett. The money is yours. Here, I have it upon me now. (takes wallet out and gives her £40)

FOOZLE (to TOMMY) My suspicions increase with every word you speak. I believe we should join forces.

TOMMY Let us wait and follow this curious barber.

FOOZLE You are right. We must have evidence before we act.

MRS LOVETT (to TODD) Another drink, Mr Todd? I am overwhelmed by this change of heart. A gift of £40!

TODD (aside) She will not live to spend it. Ha haaaaaaa!

CUSTOMER 1 (rising) Gentlemen! The Queen!

(CUSTOMERS all stand.)

No! No! You misunderstand me. Gentlemen - the Queen!

(To the amazement of all QUEEN VICTORIA enters with ATTENDANT. CUSTOMERS all fall to their knees and grovel.)

VICTORIA My subjects, we are pleased with your welcome. You grovel beautifully. You may rise - respectfully.

(They do so. PICKLE enters DSL with some more wine. He does not notice VICTORIA.)

PICKLE Here you are, sir, and though I say it myself, there ain't a better bottle opened at Buck House.

VICTORIA At Buckingham Palace, sir, one uses this substance for the shampooing of the Royal Corgis.

PICKLE (throwing himself on the floor) Oh, forgive me, your Majesty.... I did not notice you there.

VICTORIA You did not notice us! Are you blind, sir? Does not our magnificence fill the room? We are most insulted by your words.

PICKLE Oh, your Majesty!

(He grovels even more. GROVEL enters DSR.)

GROVEL Are you all right, Mr Pickle? Who's the old crow?

VICTORIA Ooooooh!

(She faints and is caught by her ATTENDANT.)

PICKLE Oh, Grovel, be quiet. Oh your Majesty forgive him. Grovel, come here. This is Her Gracious Majesty Queen Victoria.

(GROVEL is impressed.)

Well don't just stand there, Grovel. Grovel.

GROVEL Grovel grovel?

PICKLE Yes, grovel Grovel!

(GROVEL grovels.)

VICTORIA (recovering) Oh this is really insufferable! One knew one would hate these new-fangled walkabouts. One should never have listened to that unspeakable Mr Gladstone.

PICKLE May I welcome you to my humble establishment, your Majesty. I am Beaujolais Pickle.

VICTORIA We sympathise. We knew your brother, Branston.

PICKLE Might I ask the reason for your doing me the honour of visiting my humble, lowly, modest er ... paltry er ....

VICTORIA Insignificant?

PICKLE ..... insignificant establishment?

VICTORIA We are following the advice of our Prime Minister, Mr Gladstone. We are advised that we should try to improve our image. We are attempting to win back the affection of the British Public.

CUSTOMER 3 Ladies and Gentlemen! The Queen!

CUSTOMERS (toasting) THE QUEEN!

VICTORIA We are pleased. We remarked to Mr Gladstone that our image was in excellent condition but the irritating fellow insisted on our putting on these clothes and visiting the haunts of some of the lower orders, the common people, the slum-dwellers and the riff-raff, the vulgar herd, the great unwashed, the humble, the servile and the base.

PICKLE (sincerely) Oh, thank you, your Majesty.

GROVEL Most kind, most kind.

TODD Ladies and Gentlemen, let us pay tribute to our most gracious and noble Queen and to the glorious empire over which she rules. May I say, your Majesty, in the words of your distinguished grandfather -
'Born and educated in this country
I glory in the name of Briton.'

(VICTORIA is escorted to a seat by TODD as they all cheer.)

MUSIC 8 Queen and Empire

TODD Drink, drink a health to the Queen.

Drink and toast the Empire.
Drink to Britain standing supreme.
OTHER NATIONS RETIRE!

VICTORIA — Drink, drink a health to me.
Drink and toast my Empire.
Drink to Britain noble and free,
Other nations admire.

MRS LOVETT — On British strength and British skill
The world is pleased and proud to lean;
And in far-flung lands the natives thrill
To the name of our great and glorious Queen!

ALL — Victoria, Victoria,
Victoria, Victoria,
Your Empire long shall last!
Victoria, Victoria,
Victoria, Victoria,
Your beauty is unsurpassed!

TODD — The world is full of beauties rare,
Of mountains grand and valleys green.
But no earthly splendours can compare
With those of our own magnificent Queen.

ALL — CHORUS

(TODD stands on chair and recites the poem. The CUSTOMERS etc. hum the tune in the background.)

TODD — This country bears a world known name
Though it is but a little spot.
I say 'tis first in the scroll of fame
And who shall say it is not?
Of the deathless ones who shine and live
In arms, in arts, or song,
The brightest the whole wide world can give
To this little land belong.
'tis the star of earth, deny it who can
The island home of an Englishman.

MRS LOVETT — In heaven's eye who can deny
That Britain stands and stands alone,

In pride of place the supreme race
All others are in shadow thrown.

ALL CHORUS

(During the final part of the song Union Jacks appear in every possible corner of the stage. They sprout from the walls and hang from the ceiling. Everyone on stage waves at least two. A patriotic tableau is formed with VICTORIA as its centre-piece.)

ALL

On yonder height what golden light
Triumphant shines and shines alone?
Unrivall'd blaze! The nations gaze!
'tis not the sun, 'tis Britain's throne.

On which the sun, on which the sun,
On which the sun, on which the sun,
On which the sun, the sun, the sun,
The sun, the sun, the sun, the sun,
On which the bright and glorious
Queen Victorious,
Bright and glorious,
Queen Victorious
Su-un
Never sets!

BLACKOUT

<u>MUSIC 9</u> <u>Rule Britannia</u>

(A spirited rendition plays as the curtains close.)

END OF ACT ONE

ACT II

Scene 1 Fleet Street

MRS LOVETT's Pie Shop USL, TODD's Barber Shop USR. Stage is bare. After a moment MRS LOVETT comes out of the shop and hangs a notice on the door: 'NEXT BATCH OF PIES READY IN TEN MINUTES'. The CITIZENS come on in ones and twos. They look at the notice and at their watches. MRS LOVETT goes back into Pie Shop.

MUSIC 10 Pies!

CITIZENS — If you want to know the reason for our sighs -
it's pies!
When we say we love them we aren't telling lies -
love pies!

CITIZEN 1 — When this aroma's in the air my stomach cries -
CITIZENS — for pies!
CITIZEN 1 — They're delicious in whatever shape and size -
CITIZENS — are pies!

CITIZENS — Pies! Pies!
We'll always love them right or wrong.
Pies! Pies!
The inspiration for our song.
Pies! Pies!
A finer feast you never saw.
Pies! Pies!
We eat them and we cry for more!

CITIZEN 2 — Our devotion to their taste we can't disguise -
CITIZENS — these pies!
CITIZEN 2 — You should follow our example if you're wise -
CITIZENS — eat pies!
CITIZEN 3 — Their superiority no one denies -
CITIZENS — meat pies!
CITIZEN 3 — To sing their praises hear our voices rise -
CITIZENS — these pies!

CITIZENS — CHORUS

(CITIZEN 4 has a hysterical fit and falls to the floor. The others crowd round her. MRS LOVETT sticks her head out of the shop door. No one sees her.)

MRS LOVETT The customers are gathered round like flies -
for pies.
But for each new batch another victim dies -
my pies!

(She goes in and brings out a tray of pies which she sells during the following verse.)

CITIZENS She's an addict; you can see it in her eyes -
for pies.
She can't give them up no matter how she tries -
these pies!

(They eat pies and sing a final chorus at the same time, spraying the stage and the first three rows with crumbs.)

Pies! Pies!
We'll always love them right or wrong.
Pies! Pies!
The inspiration for our song!
Pies! Pies!
A finer feast you never saw.
Pies! Pies!
We eat them and we cry for more!

CITIZEN 1 Mrs Lovett, your meat pies are the finest I have ever tasted.

CITIZEN 2 I would give a lot to know the recipe for your delicious gravy.

MRS LOVETT Oh, ma'am, that is a well kept secret indeed.

CITIZEN 3 What I like about your pies is that they have so much ..... so much ... so much body in them.

(MRS LOVETT gives him a look.)

CITIZEN 4 (laughing) Perhaps - perhaps that - perhaps that is the secret ingredient - bodies.

(They all laugh uproariously. MRS LOVETT looks most alarmed.)

CITIZEN 1 Is that your dark secret, Mrs Lovett?

(They all laugh again. MRS LOVETT decides to make the best of it.)

MRS LOVETT I see I am beaten, my friends. Indeed you have hit upon it. My pies indeed contain ... human flesh.

(They all laugh heartily.)

Yours, sir, contains a portion of my mother-in-law.

(Louder laughter.)

And yours, ma'am, certain pieces of the late Archbishop of Canterbury.

(They are by now screaming with laughter.)

MUSIC 11 Secret Recipe

MRS LOVETT I'd been making pies for twenty years -
CITIZENS years.
MRS LOVETT My business though was not a great success,
Then I made a change that ended all the sneers -
CITIZENS sneers.
MRS LOVETT And now to you my secret I'll confess.

It ain't veal, it ain't steak, it ain't ham,
You'll never guess.
It ain't beef, it ain't pork, it ain't lamb,
It's human flesh!
And now my secret recipe
Has made a wealthy woman of me,
'cos everyone's into my pies -
Everyone's into my pies!

MRS LOVETT For years I tried experiments with pastry -
CITIZENS pastry.

MRS LOVETT — I made it short and flaky, choux and puff.
Then I thought of how to make the meat more tasty -
CITIZENS — tasty.
MRS LOVETT — And now my clients just can't get enough!

ALL — CHORUS

MRS LOVETT — So now I've solved my old financial problem -
CITIZENS — problem.
MRS LOVETT — Pie fillings come here on their own two feet,
And once inside, of course, I kill and rob them -
CITIZENS — rob them!
MRS LOVETT — They meet their maker and then I make meat!

ALL — CHORUS

CITIZENS — She'd been making pies for twenty years -
MRS LOVETT — years!
CITIZENS — Her business, though, was not a great success.
Then she made a change that ended all the sneers -
MRS LOVETT — sneers!
CITIZENS — And now to you her secret she's confessed!

ALL — CHORUS

(MRS LOVETT goes back into her shop and the CITIZENS leave the stage. TODD enters from his shop and speaks to the audience:)

TODD — Gathering clouds warn the mountaineer of the approaching storm. Let them now warn me to provide against danger. I have too many enemies to be safe. I will dispose of them one by one until no evidence of my guilt remains. My first step must be to stop the babbling tongue of Tobias Stoutheart. Mrs Lovett, too, grows scrupulous and dissatisfied. I've had my eye on her for some time and I fear she intends mischief.

(TOMMY, FOOZLE and ORLANDO enter USL behind TODD.)

A little poison skilfully administered may remove any unpleasantness in that quarter. Ha ha haaaa- (laugh is cut off, hears noise behind) Who's there?

FOOZLE Sweeney Todd! Where is my master?

TODD How should I know, imbecile?

TOMMY Sweeney Todd! Where is my shipmate?

TODD Why do you ask me, you nautical nitwit?

(ORLANDO barks at TODD.)

Be gone, you overfed whippet!

(ORLANDO attacks TODD.)

Get him off me. Why do you dog my footsteps?

(ORLANDO and TODD fight.)

How dare you hound me in this way! (fight continues)

TOMMY I am in no doubt that this man has committed some unspeakable crime.

FOOZLE I fear, friend, that our companions may be dead.

TOMMY If that be so may I not see salt water again if I do not bring this man to justice. Let us bide our time. We must find evidence to support our suspicions.

FOOZLE Orlando! Come!

(ORLANDO stops attacking TODD.)

Be sure, sir, that you will not continue with your evil plans.

TODD Ha ha haaaaaa! Who shall stop me?

FOOZLE If Heaven gives me power, I shall.

(Exit TODD laughing hysterically to MRS LOVETT's shop. TOMMY, FOOZLE and ORLANDO exeunt DSR.)

BLACKOUT

Scene 2 The Bakehouse in MRS LOVETT's cellar

(It is dark and spooky. A table with drawer USL, a piece of wall with a hidden entrance USR next to a door leading to the ovens, and a large piece of machinery draped in sacking USC. Door to shop DSL. MRS LOVETT drags ANGELO on DSL.)

ANGELO Oh, signora, why you kip me lockeda ina da cellar here?

MRS LOVETT Stop whining, boy. We have work to do.

ANGELO Not more pies!

MRS LOVETT Yes, of course more pies. Business is very good today. Fetch me the latest batch from the ovens.

(Exit ANGELO USR.)

It seems the boy does not yet suspect anything. I will keep him under lock and key to be sure.

(ANGELO returns in distress, carrying a pie.)

ANGELO Ooooh, signora! Isa hot! Here, signora!

(He hands the hot pie to MRS LOVETT.)

MRS LOVETT Don't give it to me, fool. Ow! (hands it back)

ANGELO (running around madly) Ow! Ooooh! Signora!

(ANGELO throws the pie from one side of the stage to the other. MRS LOVETT catches it, DSR.)

MRS LOVETT Ow! Open that drawer, quickly!

(ANGELO turns and opens drawer in table USL. MRS LOVETT runs over and drops the pie into the drawer. Drawer has no bottom and the pie crashes to the floor.)

Fetch the <u>cool</u> pies from the bakehouse, stupid boy!

(Exit ANGELO USR. MRS LOVETT clears up the mess. ANGELO returns with an enormous stack of pies ten feet high which wobbles alarmingly.)

Be careful, boy!

(ANGELO runs around the stage almost tipping the pies on to MRS LOVETT and the audience. Finally he can maintain the balance no longer and the stack slowly tips over towards MRS LOVETT. Just before it hits the ground MRS LOVETT catches the top pie and she and ANGELO hold the stack between them.)

Take them to the shop!

(ANGELO tucks the stack under one arm and takes them out DSL. MRS LOVETT yawns.)

I'm not getting enough sleep. If only I could sleep - without dreaming.

(ANGELO returns.)

Now we must prepare the next batch of pies.

ANGELO (groaning) Is a no end to the work. Avanti vermicelli ....

MRS LOVETT (grabbing him by the ear) What do you say, boy? Am I not a kind and considerate employer?

ANGELO Si signora. (released) Rigatoni spumanti!

MRS LOVETT (giving him a look) I am such a kind and considerate employer that I have purchased at enormous expense - £40 - a new invention from your own native land which will revolutionise the pie-making industry - here! (uncovers the large piece of machinery USC) The Pastriacci Pie-making Machine Mark III!

ANGELO Oh signora! E bellissima!

MRS LOVETT And beautiful, too.

ANGELO — How does it worka?

MRS LOVETT — I have the instruction booklet, here. This is where you will be useful. The instructions are all in Italian. You must translate.

ANGELO — (taking the book, reads:) 'IMPORTANT NOTICE — The makers accept no responsibility for any injuries or deaths which may occur as a result of using the Pastriacci Mark III.'

MRS LOVETT — Never mind that! What is the first thing we have to do?

ANGELO — The firsta thing it say .... 'Plug it in'.

MRS LOVETT — Plug it in? Plug it in?! What are you talking about? Have you no sense of time? It is 1853!

ANGELO — (looking at his watch) No, signora, it isa ten past nine. It say here, signora, 'plug it in'.

(MRS LOVETT shrugs and plugs it in.)

MRS LOVETT — Right. What's next?

ANGELO — 'Put in the ingredients'.

MRS LOVETT — The ingredients. Ah, yes...., (picks up a large bag labelled 'FLOUR' and throws it in the top of the machine - bag and all) Fetch some water, Angelo.

(ANGELO exits DSL. Whilst he is gone MRS LOVETT produces a 'human' leg and other items on a tray from the bakehouse and throws these in. ANGELO returns with a jug of water - not necessarily full - which is poured into the machine from the side.)

Now what?

ANGELO — 'Select your programme.'

MRS LOVETT — 'Programme'?

ANGELO Si signora. On the dial here. You choose-a the size of the pie.

MRS LOVETT Ah, yes. A medium size one, I think. Right. Next?

ANGELO 'Switch on'.

MRS LOVETT (doing so) Switch on.

(Dials whirl. An extraordinary bubbling and fizzing noise is heard. A pie shoots out of a hole in the machine - not the side on which they are standing - and smashes on the floor.)

ANGELO (reading) 'Be a ready to receive the pie at window A'.

MRS LOVETT Now you tell me! Look at that!

ANGELO Try again, signora. Press the switch.

MRS LOVETT Press the switch. (she hurries to window A - this time the pie shoots out of the top and hits her on the head) I should have known better than to buy an Italian machine. It takes after you. It doesn't work! (kicks the machine angrily)

ANGELO (still reading) Warning! Never - repeat never - kicka da machine!

(The machine begins to work, a few pies shoot out of the holes in the sides and one comes out of the top. It builds up to a crescendo of weird noises and an enormous explosion. The machine falls apart revealing the OPERATOR inside, black-faced and singed looking. He walks over to MRS LOVETT carrying a bag of flour, and snatching book from ANGELO reads:)

OPERATOR 'Garibaldi risorgimento minestrone suppa inglese.' You no read? Never - repeat-a never - kicka da machine!

(He dumps the bag of flour on MRS LOVETT's head and storms out DSL.)

MRS LOVETT (coughing) This is all your fault. Clean up this mess. (exit DSL)

ANGELO (picking up pies and putting the machine back together) Oh how I wish I was back in Napoli - the wine, the musica, the sunshine .... the spaghetti! Zis place I am bullied. It isa miserable life. See, here ina da cellar there is nothing visible buta da darkness. I think it woulda be quite unbearable if it wasn't fora da delicious odour ofa da pies. Eh, anda talking ofa da pies, I fancy I coulda eat one! (takes one off the pile he has collected and eats it greedily) Bellissima! Deliciosa! Lots a da gravy! (he suddenly discovers a long hair, views it with puzzlement and winds it round his finger) Somebody's been combing their hair. I no thinka thata pie is a nice one. (he puts part of the eaten pie back and takes another) Thatsa better ... buta no ... Whata have we here? A bone? No, a button ... and what .. no ... Santa Maria! ... no ... si .... it isa ... ugh! A fingernail! How did a fingernail come into a pie? Angelo no feel well. (looks around nervously) There isa something funny going on here.

MUSIC 12 <u>Something Funny Going on Here</u>

ANGELO There's something strange
In this place.
I sense there's danger
In this place,
I somehow fear
Evil is near.
Isa something funny going on here

(Lights dim and several GHOSTS appear, including that of ALONZO, who looks very put out at the company he is keeping.)

GHOST 1 I came 'ere for an 'aircut.
She popped me in 'er pastry.
You 'ave me in your 'and there,
I 'ope you find me tasty!

(ANGELO drops the pie he's holding.)

GHOST 2

I was Todd's first victim,
They used to call me Sidney.
'E made me into meat pies,
Now I'm steak and kidney!

(Apart from ALONZO the GHOSTS all join up to do a jolly cockney-style knees-up dance to the chorus.)

ALL

Lor' luv a duck, sir. Oh, cor blimey!
I wish I'd let me beard grow. I wish I'd been wise.
What a way to end up - as perishin' pie meat -
This homicidal barber cuts his clients down to pies.

GHOST 3

She made me into baked meat
And sold me to me wife.
She said she'd never 'ad such
Indigestion in 'er life!

GHOST 4

We wanted our revenge so
We took a tip from 'amlet.
We've given you the info
But do you understand yet?

ALL

Lor' luv a duck, sir. Oh, cor blimey!
As a barber and a butcher he'll be numbered with the best.
We may have 'ad to end up as perishin' pie meat
But when he slits your throat it is a cut above the chest!

ANGELO

Dread apparitions
I'm on my knees.
Grant me remission,
Don't kill me please.
I somehow fear
My end isa near.
Isa something funny going on here!

ALONZO

We'd like to see his capture,
We cannot rest without it.
It's not that we are spiteful -
But we feel cut up about it!

GHOST 6

So now it's up to you,son,

We hope you'll lend a hand.
They might think us insubstantial
If we took the witness stand!

(For the final chorus all the GHOSTS including ALONZO - albeit reluctantly - join in the dance.)

ALL

Lor' luv a duck, sir, Oh, cor blimey!
After what he did to us we never can forgive him.
What a way to end up as perishin' pie meat!
If you ask him why he'll tell you IT'S TO CUT THE
COST OF LIVING!

(GHOSTS exeunt L and R dancing. ANGELO hides his head, quaking.)

ANGELO

These are da murdered ghosts come to aska for their bodies - and they are amade into da pies! Plis, it no me! I no know what happen! (looks up nervously) Oh da holy saints be praised. They are gone.

(The wall behind him starts to open. He screams and runs out USR. TOBIAS appears knocking bricks out of the wall and climbs in carrying a sailor hat.)

TOBIAS

At last I fancy I have got to the bottom of the mystery. This passage connects Mr Todd's barber shop with next door, and here he must dispose of his victims - but this is the cellar of Mrs Lovett's Pie Shop. She too must have a part in this murderous business - and murder is indeed the word! I have discovered, in the cellar of Todd's shop, this hat belonging to the sailor whom Todd shaved this morning. He has not returned to claim it. (sniffs) I fear he never will. I shall search here in Mrs Lovett's cellar for further evidence. I am resolved to bring this murderer to justice. (looks behind table) Merciful Heavens! (looks down again and then steps to the front of the stage) The very man of whom I spoke! The handsome sailor who visited the shop today - dead! (sniffs) His naked body lies in yonder corner. I must be quick. A policeman!

BILLY (off) Oooooh!

TOBIAS But hold! (dashes back to the table, looks down and dashes back to the front of the stage) He stirs! (dashes back to table and then forward again) He lives! (dashes back and helps BILLY up) Thank heavens!

(BILLY's head appears above the back of the table. He is holding it painfully. TOBIAS dashes R and picks up a piece of sacking.)

Here, wrap yourself in this until we can restore your uniform to you.

(BILLY turns his back on the audience and wraps the sacking round his waist. Every inch of flesh visible is covered with tattoos. As he turns and shows his chest the name 'SUSAN' is clearly visible.)

BILLY Oh, my head! Thank you, boy.

TOBIAS You have a great many tattoos, sir.

BILLY Indeed. I am every inch a sailor.

TOBIAS Yes, I noticed that. (reading) 'Susan'. (wistfully) Your sweetheart, sir?

BILLY The most wonderful lady in the world - and I have seen the world, boy. Now, we must act quickly. This evil barber must be brought to justice. I am inclined to challenge him myself. A fight to the death.

TOBIAS (her admiration growing by the second) You fear not death, sir?

BILLY Death? No! Since first I trod the Queen's oak he has been about me. I have slept near him, watched near him. He has looked upon my face and saw I shrunk not. In the storm I have heeded him not. In the fury of the battle I have not thought of him - (change of tone) But, quickly, boy, how do we escape from this dingy charnel-house?

TOBIAS We must return through this wall to Todd's shop. From there we can make our way to the Bow Street Police Station.

BILLY But I cannot walk in public dressed like this.

TOBIAS You are right. You must be dressed more decently. Here.

(She hands him his sailor's hat.)

BILLY Ah, that's better! Let us waste no time.

MUSIC 13

TOBIAS No. We'll go straight after this song.

Turn Them In

TOBIAS & BILLY
We've discovered the construction of this evil operation.
They must be punished for their direful sin.
The black history of their murders makes a gruesome recitation,
And now we're going to turn them in.

Turn them, turn them, turn them in.
We'll be the heroes of the day!
Turn them, turn them, turn them in.
We'll show them that their crime can't pay!

TOBIAS For years they must have murdered and robbed without detection -
BILLY It's time their business was brought to a stop!
TOBIAS Their crimes must be reported 'cos the public needs protection -
BILLY They'll both be sentenced to the drop!

TOBIAS & BILLY
Turn them, turn them, turn them in.
We'll be the heroes of the day!
Turn them, turn them, turn them in.
We'll show them that their crime can't pay!

(At the end of the chorus TODD and MRS LOVETT

enter through the wall USR, creep behind TOBIAS and BILLY and knock them out.)

TODD & MRS LOVETT
They've discovered the construction of our evil operation.
It was fortunate that we came in.
It was imperative that we should interrupt their celebration -
For they were going to turn us in!

Turn us, turn us, turn us in!
They'll be sorry they came here today.
Turn us, turn us, turn us in,
We'll show them that our crime can pay!

(They repeat the chorus doing a celebratory dance.)

MRS LOVETT They know our secret, Mr Todd. We shall have to dispose of them. (draws finger across her throat)

TODD No, no, Mrs Lovett. Simply tie them up. There are other ways of silencing them.

MRS LOVETT Other ways?

TODD I have a very good friend ....

(MRS LOVETT laughs uproariously.)

..... (scowling) I repeat. I have a very good friend by the name of Mr Napoleon Bedlam. He is the warden of the public asylum at Peckham.

MRS LOVETT The madhouse in Peckham?

TODD Exactly so.

MRS LOVETT Of what use is a madhouse keeper to us?

TODD (laughing hysterically) Do you not see? Shortly he will have two more inmates. (starts tying up BILLY)

MRS LOVETT (tying up TOBIAS) I see but can we trust him?

TODD (aside) You, my friend, cannot trust me. A few shillings will be sufficient to stop his mouth. Right, quickly now. Take the boy. I will deal with the sailor.

(They drag the unfortunate BILLY and TOBIAS off DSL. ANGELO appears from the bakehouse USR, and exit through wall into TODD's shop.)

BLACKOUT

Scene 3 The Madhouse at Peckham

(The Madhouse is a dark and dismal place, with doors DSL, USL and USR. A large substantial table DSR on which there is a large padlocked box. On the wall USC is the inscription 'QUIS CUSTODIET IPSOS CUSTODES?' The table also has an enormous book lying on it, and NAPOLEON BEDLAM sitting at it. He opens the book and scribbles in it. Then he unlocks the box and counts the contents - it is full of gold coins.)

BEDLAM How pleasant it is to hear the sound of gold. The very word is music. Gold. Gold. Gold. Gold. (stands in excitement) Gold. I love it! I want more. Gold! Ha ha ha ha. (pauses and notices audience) This is a madhouse..... I know what you're thinking, You think I am mad. I am the keeper of this establishment. There is no one here who would dare to call me mad. No, indeed. The inmates know me. They fear to arouse my anger. They know better than to annoy me. They know that here I have complete power over them. The law cannot protect them here. Within these walls I control all. Supreme power is mine! Ha ha ha ha! (as his hysteria increases he climbs onto the table) No one dare challenge my authority. I am like a god! Indeed to these miserable creatures I am a god. A god almighty. Ha ha ha ha ha ha!

(As BEDLAM jumps up and down on the table screaming, so TODD enters USR behind him. Aware that

BEDLAM does not realise he is in the room TODD coughs. BEDLAM turns and is highly embarrassed by his appearance. He climbs down from the table.)

Mr Sweeney Todd, I think, if my memory don't deceive me?

TODD You are right, Napoleon Bedlam. I believe I am not easily forgotten by those who have once seen me.

BEDLAM True, sir. You are not easily forgotten. What can I do for you now?

TODD I am rather unfortunate with my boys. I have two here who have shown such decided symptoms of insanity that it becomes, I regret to say, absolutely necessary to place them under your care.

BEDLAM Indeed? Do they rave?

TODD Oh yes they do, and about the most absurd nonsense in the world. To hear them one would really think that, instead of being one of the most humane of men, I was, in point of fact, an absolute murderer.

BEDLAM A murderer?

TODD Could anything be more absurd than such an accusation?

BEDLAM For how long do you think that this malady will continue?

TODD I will pay for twelve months but I do not think, between you and I, that the case will last anything like so long. I think they will die like Simkins - suddenly!

(They both laugh madly.)

BEDLAM I shouldn't wonder if they did. You may as well introduce me to your patients at once.

TODD I shall have great pleasure in showing them to you. (calls off) Mrs Lovett, would you bring in the victims er, the patients, please?

(MRS LOVETT enters USR leading BILLY and TOBIAS still tied up.)

BEDLAM Ah, I see that they are quite young.

TODD Yes, more's the pity.

BEDLAM' On the contrary, they will be most popular with the audience.

MRS LOVETT (looking at the audience) With the audience?

TODD Not <u>that</u> audience.

BEDLAM No, indeed, ma'am.

MRS LOVETT What audience then?

TODD Mr Bedlam raises money for the upkeep of this establishment by allowing the public to visit the asylum - for a small charge.

BEDLAM The public have a great curiosity on the subject of madness. We try to satisfy that curiosity. If we also make a little money, heh, heh, so much the better!

MRS LOVETT You mean the public just come in and <u>watch</u> the lunatics?

TODD In a way. But they do not see them simply running wild. Mr Bedlam trains them.

MRS LOVETT Trained lunatics?

BEDLAM Perhaps you would understand better if I were to give you a sample of their performance.

TODD Oh, no, no. Do not put yourself to such trouble.

BEDLAM No trouble, sir. (rings bell) They will be here directly.

TODD (to MRS LOVETT) You and your questions! Now we shall both have to suffer.

(From the dark door USL a number of half naked, ragged, unkempt creatures shamble towards the front of the stage. They are lit only by blue lights. Some come DSR behind MRS LOVETT who is startled and runs to hide behind BEDLAM.)

BEDLAM There is no need for fear, ma'am. They are perfectly harmless - except for Enoch.

ENOCH Grrrrrrrr!

BEDLAM I would introduce you but it would be useless.

MRS LOVETT Useless? Why?

BEDLAM Let me demonstrate. (to INMATE 1) Good evening.

INMATE 1 Boots, boots, boots, boots, boots, boots, boots -

BEDLAM (striking him) Your name?

INMATE 1 I am Napoleon Bonaparte. (strikes a Napoleon pose)

BEDLAM Indeed? And who told you that?

INMATE 1 God. God told me.

INMATE 2 I did no such thing!

(INMATES 1 and 2 fight. BEDLAM beats them apart.)

BEDLAM You see conversation is useless, but there is one way in which they can express themselves. My visitors usually find it - amusing.

MRS LOVETT What way is that?

BEDLAM It is a form of singing ... er ... music.

MRS LOVETT A <u>form</u> of music?

BEDLAM I have given it the name of <u>rock</u> music.

TODD Why rock music?

BEDLAM When it's over you feel like you've been hit by a rock! Stand clear, please. I would not like you to be injured during the performance. We begin with a little mathematics. Right, pay attention, (coughs) counting begin.

INMATE 1 One.

INMATE 2 Two.

INMATE 3 Five.

INMATE 4 Eight.

BEDLAM No, no, no. Again. Counting - begin!

INMATE 1 One.

INMATE 2 One.

BEDLAM No, <u>two</u>.

INMATE 3 Two.

BEDLAM No, you're three, he's two.

INMATE 4 He's thirty five if he's a day.

BEDLAM No, no, NO! (to TODD and MRS LOVETT) This won't take a moment. (to INMATES) Repeat after me. One.

INMATES One.

BEDLAM Two.

INMATES Two.

BEDLAM Three.

INMATES Three.

BEDLAM Four.

INMATES Four.

BEDLAM Now we're getting somewhere.

INMATES Now we're getting somewhere.

BEDLAM (embarrassed) Ha ha ha.

INMATES Ha ha ha.

BEDLAM No, no, no.

INMATES No, no, no.

BEDLAM Stop it!

INMATES Stop it!

BEDLAM I'll thrash the next -

INMATES I'll thrash the next -

(BEDLAM screams. The INMATES scream. BEDLAM now cunningly remains silent. He walks around the line of INMATES like a sergeant-major.)

BEDLAM Repeat after me.

INMATES Repeat after me.

BEDLAM One, two, three, four.

INMATES One, two, three, four.

BEDLAM One, two, three, four.

INMATES One, two, three, four.

BEDLAM One, two, three, four.

INMATES One, two, three, four.

(This last count leads into MUSIC 14 Each INMATE produces a microphone. They dance frantically. Coloured lights and a strobe add to the excitement.)

Crazy

INMATES

Look around, see our plight.
Locked in here out of sight.
In our padded cells confined,
We are all out of our minds.

Pity our misery,
Victims of society.
Kept in dungeons here below -
Every day another show!

We don't care if they all say we're crazy!
We don't care if they all say we're crazy!
We don't care if they all say we're crazy!
Yeah!

Every day there's a chance
To see our madman's dance.
Every step that we complete
Jolts our wits into our feet!

Every day people throng
To hear our madman's song.
Looney tunes from every throat
Paranoia in each note!

CHORUS

Wouldn't it break your hearts?
We are all Bonapartes.
We, the Emperors of France
Here are forced to sing and dance.

But admit that it's true
We have fun, more than you.
Pleasures sure from madness grow,
Which none but we madmen know.

CHORUS

(During the song TOBIAS and BILLY have been struggling with their ropes. TOBIAS has managed to remove her gag.)

TOBIAS (shouting) Sweeney Todd is a murderer and I denounce him!

TODD You hear him?

BEDLAM Mad indeed.

MRS LOVETT Could anyone but a maniac make so absurd an assertion?

BEDLAM No, it is insanity in its most terrible form. I see I shall have to put him in a strait-waistcoat.

TODD I'm afraid mild treatment, which I have tried, only irritates the disease. Therefore I must leave you, as a professional, to deal with the case as seems fit.

MRS LOVETT But time presses on, Mr Todd, and I have no doubt the patients will be properly attended to.

(They start to leave, shaking hands with BEDLAM.)

TODD (to TOBIAS) Ha haaaa! How do you feel now? Do you still think I shall hang or will you die in the cell of a madhouse? (to audience) Do you see, my friends, how evil will always triumph over weak, wishy-washy goodness and kindness? Ha ha haaaaaa!

(TODD and MRS LOVETT leave USR.)

BILLY Ummmm. Urgle, urle, urgle.

(BEDLAM removes his gag.)

I don't know who you are, sir, but let me beg you to have the house of Sweeney Todd, in Fleet Street, searched and you will find that he is a murderer.

TOBIAS There are at least a hundred watches, rings, trinkets and other belongings of the unfortunate persons who have met their deaths through him.

BEDLAM How uncommonly mad! (rings the bell - two KEEPERS enter) You will take these new inmates under your care. They seem extremely unsettled and feverish. Shave their heads and put strait-waistcoats on them. Let them be conveyed to one of the dark, damp cells as too much light will encourage their wild delirium.

BILLY We will die before we submit to you!

BEDLAM Then die! For no power can aid you!

TOBIAS Yes, there is one - Heaven - which fails not to succour the helpless and the persecuted.

(BILLY has been struggling with his ropes, now with one mighty bound he is free!)

BILLY Now, sir, we meet on equal terms. (frees TOBIAS)

BEDLAM Quickly fools, restrain them.

(An enormous fight takes place between TOBIAS, BILLY and BEDLAM and the two KEEPERS. At first the INMATES just watch.)

BILLY Come my friends! This is your chance to be free from this vile and accursed prison.

(The INMATES join in the fight carrying off BEDLAM and the two KEEPERS USL.)

Free! Let us go quickly - Bow Street!

(TOBIAS and BILLY exeunt USR.)

Scene 4 Fleet Street

(MRS LOVETT's Pie Shop USL, TODD's Barber Shop USR. TODD and MRS LOVETT enter DSR cross stage sniggering and enter the Pie Shop. They are followed a moment later by the POLICE CONSTABLE.)

CONSTABLE Evening all. I think I hear footsteps. (pause - nothing happens, he looks into wings and repeats louder:) I THINK I HEAR FOOTSTEPS!

(FOOZLE, TOMMY and ORLANDO run on stage from one side, BILLY and TOBIAS from the other. BILLY is now fully dressed in what ever he has persuaded the INMATES and TOBIAS to give him.)

FOOZLE (to CONSTABLE) Come quickly!

CONSTABLE What seems to be the trouble?

(They all gabble incomprehensibly for ten seconds finishing in perfect unison:)

Just as I thought, but ...?

(They gabble again. ORLANDO bounds around madly.)

Ah, I see. Does that mean ....?

(They gabble again ending together with:)

ALL The Pie Shop! (all point at the door)

CONSTABLE The unspeakable fiend!

FOOZLE What are we to do?

BILLY A brilliant idea!

FOOZE Yes?

TOBIAS Yes?

BILLY That's what we need - a brilliant idea.

CONSTABLE In a case like this there is only one thing to do -

ALL What?

CONSTABLE Stand back! With one blast on this whistle I will summon .... the Dwarf Squad!

ALL The Dwarf Squad?

CONSTABLE Observe!

(He blows the whistle. Six POLICEMEN march on and line up. They can either be the six smallest members of the cast or the six largest - on their knees with dummy shoes attached!)

ALL Amazing!

FOOZLE It's a sort of teeny weeny Sweeney.

POLICEMEN Evenin' all, 'ello, 'ello, 'ello. What's all this 'ere then? Mind how you go.

TOBIAS (whispers) But why are they all dwarves?

CONSTABLE They're specially trained for dealing with low criminals.

FOOZLE Little doubt.

TOMMY Small wonder.

CONSTABLE Dwarf Constables, atten - SHUN!

(They come smartly to attention.)

At the double .... wait for it ... to the Barber's Shop!

(The CONSTABLE heads DSL, all the others rush off stage R. The CONSTABLE stops and looks back. He blows his whistle and signals to them to follow him. The others all appear again and dash across the stage knocking the CONSTABLE over and trampling on him. He gets up shakily and staggers after them. Finally after a lot of whistle blowing off stage the CONSTABLE leads the POLICEMEN, TOMMY, BILLY, TOBIAS, FOOZLE and ORLANDO USR and into TODD's shop.)

Scene 5 The Bakehouse in MRS LOVETT's cellar

(TODD and MRS LOVETT are discovered in violent argument.)

MRS LOVETT My mind is made up, Mr Todd. I will no longer have anything to do with this evil business. I cannot sleep without dreaming of our countless victims, our brutal crimes. Horrible nightmares!

TODD It is too late for you to be troubled with a conscience. (aside) The time has come to dispose of this pompous pie-maker.

MRS LOVETT May God forgive me for my sins! (aside) One final murder and I shall be safe. (shows the audience her hidden knife)

TODD Come, come. We have been friends these many years. Let us not quarrel now.

MRS LOVETT You are right, of course, Mr Todd. It is as you say, Mr Todd, friends, the greatest of friends.

TODD Thick as thieves, Mrs Lovett.

MRS LOVETT Oh yes, certainly, Mr Todd .... thick, Mr Todd .... very thick.

(They move to opposite sides of the stage as MUSIC 15 begins:)

Thick As Thieves

MRS LOVETT You're my oldest comrade, Sweeney,
Why I'm almost like your wife.
I'll be very pleased to see you
On the sharp end of my knife!

(She throws knife at TODD, it misses and sticks in the wall with a thud. TODD does not notice.)

TODD My dear companion, I am yours,
My inseparable aide.

Her friendship may decline, of course,
When she feels my razor blade!

(He turns swinging his razor violently at the spot where he thinks MRS LOVETT is standing. She isn't there - he misses, spins and falls over. The razor skids away out of reach.)

BOTH

Thick as thieves,
Thick as thieves.
We're the greatest of friends. It'd make you sick,
Although you may think that thieves are thick
Not we -
We're thick, thick, thick, thick,
Thick, thick, thick, thick,
Thick, thick, thick, thick,
Thick as thieves!

MRS LOVETT

I have often heard the saying,
'A true friend is hard to beat'.
I know what kind of game he's playing -
You look tired, take a seat!

(She picks up a chair to smash on TODD's head, but as she swings it it falls apart and she is left holding a single leg. She smiles sweetly at TODD.)

TODD

My friend, your words have touched me,
We'll be comrades until death -
Which in her case will come shortly,
She seems somehow out of breath!

(TODD has, he thinks, thrown a cord around MRS LOVETT's neck and is fiercely strangling her. In fact the cord is around a hatstand. MRS LOVETT walks in to TODD's line of vision.He drops the cord and smiles.)

BOTH CHORUS

TODD You have a beautiful singing voice, Mrs Lovett.

MRS LOVETT Why thank you, Mr Todd.

TODD (pulling out a pistol and shooting MRS LOVETT who

falls to the ground, dead) They say the Devil has all the best tunes. He will be pleased to see you! She is gone - gone - and not a witness to the deed!

ANGELO (sticking his head through wall USR) Excepta me!

TODD (not noticing ANGELO) Dead men tell no tales! I am free! I am free! Ha ha haaaaaaa! Now let the furnace consume the body as it would wheaten straw and destroy all evidence of my guilt in this as it has in my manifold deeds of blood.

(He goes USC to MRS LOVETT's body, putting down the gun near the wall USR. ANGELO reaches in and picks it up whilst TODD is recoiling from the body.)

Those eyes! She stares at me - even in death she accuses me, but take courage. The body must be removed.

(He approaches it again, head averted. ANGELO enters USR unseen.)

ANGELO Sweeney Todd! I accuse you of murder!

TODD (screams) Oh save me! The dead accuse me! Mercy! I cry mercy! (turns and sees that it is ANGELO) It is the Italian boy! You think to frighten me, boy. I will deal swiftly with you.

(He moves towards ANGELO, who points the gun at him. TODD stops in his tracks.)

(smiling) Come, come, Angelo amico, is it to be war or peace between us?

ANGELO War! War to the last! War until I see you, signore, placed in da felon's dock anda sentenced bya da judge.

TODD Be prudent. Remember, I am now rich.

ANGELO But your reign will soon be over. What will your position be, do you think, when the world knows all?

TODD	(advancing) You foolish urchin I will -
ANGELO	Stand back or I willa shoot.
	(TODD advances, ANGELO pulls the trigger but the gun is empty. TODD laughs and dives for him. At this moment, just in the nick of time, the door DSL bursts open and in march the CONSTABLE, POLICEMEN, TOMMY, BILLY, TOBIAS, FOOZLE and ORLANDO.)
CONSTABLE	Sweeney Todd, I arrest you in the name of Her Imperial Majesty Queen Victoria. Restrain him!
	(The POLICEMEN grab TODD. He is handcuffed to the tiniest.)
TOBIAS	Now Sweeney Todd you shall hang for your wicked crimes!
BILLY	You were a fool to think that you could escape.
FOOZLE	Now Londoners will be safe from your cut-throat razor.
TOMMY	All thanks to the dwarf squad.
ANGELO	I thinka your British Policemen are awonderful.
CONSTABLE	Why, thank you. We do our best, you know.
TODD	You think to arrest me? You will have to catch me first!
	(With this he dashes off through the audience heading for the back exit, dragging with him the POLICEMAN to whom he is handcuffed. There is an enormous chase through the audience, everybody shouting, whistles going off, bells ringing. The CONSTABLE fires a gun. Sirens and strobe lighting all add to the confusion. When all the cast have exited at the back of the audience TODD reappears on stage free from his handcuffs. He hides under the table USL. Seconds later his pursuers appear. They look all around.)

BILLY — He has escaped.

TOBIAS — We have let him slip from our grasp.

(The table is walking slowly across the stage.)

FOOZLE — I think not. Look! (points at table)

(They all stare at the table. BILLY and TOMMY stand on either side of it. They lift the table off TODD who continues to crawl across the stage. The POLICEMEN grab him.)

CONSTABLE — Take him away.

(TODD and POLICEMEN carry MRS LOVETT's body off.)

TOBIAS — What will happen to him, sir?

CONSTABLE — Justice will take its course.

BILLY — We shall have to wait for news.

NEWSBOY — (entering DSL and crossing stage) Extra! Extra! Sweeney Todd to hang! Extra! Extra! (exit DSR)

TOMMY — A fitting end for such a criminal.

(The POLICEMEN bring back TODD covered in chains and with a ball and chain around his ankle. He weeps and falls to his knees.)

TODD — Oh woe is me! May Heaven forgive me for my dark and foul deeds. I feared it would come to this and all through accursed gold, for which men sell their souls and barter their eternal salvation. REPENT! Repent! Truly I repent! Spare me! Spare my life, I beg you. Will no one speak for me? Just one word?

(They all turn their backs on him. NEWSBOY returns.)

NEWSBOY — Extra! Extra! Queen pardons Sweeney Todd!

ALL — (turning back) WHAT?!

NEWSBOY Queen pardons Sweeney Todd.

FOOZLE She can't do that!

VICTORIA (entering DSL) We can do whatever we like, you revolting little common person. We are the Queen. Here is our proclamation. 'It is our wish that Mr Sweeney Todd, having been found guilty of twenty-seven separate murders shall not be hanged. He shall be imprisoned for life ....'

TODD (delighted) I am spared! Thank the Lord!

VICTORIA Thank who?

TODD Thank you, your Majesty.

VICTORIA That's better ...... 'he shall be imprisoned for life in the madhouse of Mr Napoleon Bedlam at Peckham.'

TODD (his face falling) What? No! Hang me! Hang me!

VICTORIA Be quiet,you ungrateful man. Mr Bedlam has sent - under guard of course - some of his inmates to welcome you to their number.

(The INMATES rush on DSL and surround TODD.)

TODD No, no, anything but this.

ENOCH One, two, three, four.

TODD I am not mad. Ask them. (gestures to the audience) They will tell you that I'm not mad. Tell them! Tell them!

AUDIENCE (encouraged by TOBIAS) Oh yes you are.

TODD Oh no I'm not.

AUDIENCE Oh yes you are.

TODD Oh no I'm not.

AUDIENCE Oh yes you are.

TODD All right, don't start enjoying yourselves now. We've nearly finished.

ENOCH (hitting TODD) One, two, three, four.

(The INMATES take TODD USL.)

VICTORIA And now we must reward those who have brought this monster to justice. You may all have an OBE. (she produces a bag and flings medals in every direction)

BILLY I must return at once to Kent to marry my sweetheart, Susan.

TOBIAS (crossing to BILLY) Alas what will now become of me? I have no master and no money. And, alas, my name isn't Susan. (takes off her cap revealing her long hair)

ALL GASP!

(BILLY stands amazed. They look into each others eyes, romantic violins are heard - sound effects.)

BILLY You're ... you're .....

TOBIAS Yes.

BILLY No....

ALL YES!

BILLY Why you're beautiful!

(They walk towards each other and stand face to face.)

My darling. Come to my farm, marry me and let us live happily ever after.

TOBIAS Oh yes my darling.

VICTORIA One moment! What about Susan?

BILLY Susan who?

(BILLY and TOBIAS kiss.)

FOOZLE Come, Orlando, our master is dead.

(ORLANDO howls.)

(brightening) But we have his secrets. His skills will live on in me. I too shall astound the crowned heads of Europe. (looks at VICTORIA and produces a pack of cards) Your Majesty, pick a card - any card.

(FOOZLE and VICTORIA go USR and continue with the card trick.)

ANGELO That leavesa only me. I have no one, nothing. Only my holy medal of Saint Peter. (on chain round his neck)

TOMMY (coming forward and inspecting the medal) Boy, where did you get this medal?

ANGELO I have had it, signore, all my life, since I was a bambino in Napoli. My mamma she tell me that my father, he leave it for me. He die before I was born.

TOMMY I had a .. a ... a wife in Naples some twelve years since. I was forced to leave her. I left her and my unborn child the only wealth I possessed - a silver medal of Saint Peter.

(Everybody looks at everybody else!)

ANGELO Father!

TOMMY My son!

(They embrace.)

ANGELO I have found a home.

TOMMY — And wealth. That medal is of great value.

BILLY — But even better than your new found home, even better than your new found wealth you have a - New Found Land! Angelo, my shipmate Tommy is your father. You realise what this means?

ANGELO — It cannot be true.

BILLY — Yes - Angelo - you are BRITISH!

ANGELO — It is all too good to be true!

(They all cheer.)

MUSIC 16 Queen and Empire (reprise)

ALL —
In Heaven's eye who can deny
That Britain stands and stands alone?
In pride of place the supreme race.
All others are in shadow thrown.

On yonder height what golden light
Triumphant shines and shines alone?
Unrivall'd blaze the nation's gaze
'tis not the sun, 'tis Britain's throne.

On which the sun, on which the sun,
On which the sun, on which the sun,
On which the sun, the sun, the sun,
The sun, the sun, the sun, the sun,
On which the bright and glorious,
Queen Victorious,
Bright and glorious,
Queen Victorious
SU-UN
NEVER SETS!

FOOZLE — (dashing to the front of the stage) But wait! In mem ory of my poor dead master I must complete his mos famous illusion. (to VICTIM 2) If you would step u here once more, sir. Most kind, sir. Most kind!

(VICTIM 2 returns to the stage. FOOZLE fills the

hat with goo from the jug. This time there are no interruptions and VICTIM 2 puts the hat on. With a dramatic gesture FOOZLE lifts the hat and the goo covers VICTIM 2's head and face. FOOZLE is a little aghast and edges away:)

Ah ... er ... yes, well ..... congratulations. This half a bacon sandwich is yours!

(With a shriek of fury VICTIM 2 chases FOOZLE off the stage, through the audience and out of the back door. Meanwhile on stage the INMATES bring TODD forward. ENOCH whispers in the ear of the CONSTABLE.)

CONSTABLE He says that they have something to show us.

TOBIAS What can it be?

(ENOCH whispers to CONSTABLE.)

CONSTABLE They have been educating Sweeney Todd.

TOBIAS Let us see what they have taught him.

ENOCH (to TODD) One, two, three, four.

(TODD remains obstinately silent.)

ONE, TWO, THREE, FOUR!

(ENOCH raises his fist at TODD.)

TODD (miserably) One, two, three, four.

(MUSIC 17 crashes in. Everybody, including VICTORIA, dances madly. Strobe and coloured lighting effects.)

Crazy! (reprise)

ALL

Every day there's a chance
To see our madman's dance.
Every step that we complete
Jolts our wits into our feet!

Every day people throng
To hear our madman's song.
Looney tunes from every throat -
Paranoia in each note!

Don't you know that everyone is crazy!
Don't you know that everyone is crazy!
Don't you know that everyone is crazy -
Yeah!

BLACKOUT

CURTAIN

<u>MUSIC 18</u> National Anthem

Printed in England by Pindar Print Limited, Scarborough, North Yorkshire.